How to Boost Your Credit Score

Repair Your Credit and Boost Your Score Like a Pro!

Dean Baldwin

Introduction

Numbers

"If you don't take good care of your credit, then your credit won't take good care of you." — Tyler Gregory

Your credit score does not have to elicit fear or stress in your life. As you have earned this score, you have likely experienced stress surrounding the idea of keeping it high. With a high credit score, you can finance a vehicle, purchase a house, and get approved for loans. It can be hard to ignore these pressures when so much about being a financially responsible individual revolves around keeping this score high. No matter what you do, it might seem like the credit card bills keep getting higher and higher, even with on-time payments. Interest rates tend to skyrocket, leaving you with high balances. As you check your credit score, you notice that it is steadily dropping. The worry stops today. Whether you want to boost your score or repair your score, you are going to be able to achieve your goals by using proven methods that you can apply to your own life.

Without having to worry about this number any longer, you will finally earn the financial freedom that you crave. While credit scores are important to some people, most Americans do not think twice about them. If you have been ignoring your number for quite some time, consider that this knowledge can be applied in various ways. When you keep your credit score up, your interest rates will decline. This will prevent you from paying too much when you borrow money. In addition, you will be approved for higher lines of credit. This can come in handy when you need that emergency spending power. According to a study by the National Foundation for Credit Counseling (NFCC) in 2016, 44% of adults have not checked their credit score in the last year. This shows just how many people tend to ignore this topic.

According to another study, the NFCC found that some people chose not to check their credit scores because they did not believe that it would benefit them knowing this information unless they were attempting to do something credit related, such as apply for a new card or secure a loan. Only 53% of people knew that sources such as electric companies and other utility services also check credit scores. Businesses from insurance companies to cell phone companies have also been known to look into this. By looking at the bigger picture, you can see just how important credit score maintenance will become in your life.

800

I am a single father with a 7-year-old son, so financial stability has always been a priority of mine. Admittedly, I was not always familiar with my own credit score. After applying for a credit card to fund my son's Christmas, I realized that I had been misled, and it was all due to the fine print. It turns out that my interest rate of 0% was an introductory offer that was given because of the holiday season. Within three months, this interest rate jumped to a whopping 20%. I was paying more than my minimum balance, but I just could not seem to get this card paid off because the total kept growing. I was discouraged, to say the least, and I was worried about my future.

This was a turning point in my life. I wanted to liberate myself from my credit card debt. In an effort to do this, I got educated. I learned all that I could about credit, and this led me to the topic of my credit score. After seeing how important it was to maintain, I changed my priorities in life. I now run my own business out of Florida that is devoted to financial planning. It is my hope to inspire others to take control over their financial stability and to break free of all the stress and worry.

These questions do not have to be complex and impossible to answer. By breaking down the concepts in a step-by-step process, I aim to help you understand exactly what you need to do to boost or build your credit score.

Chapter 1: Death and Taxes vs. Life and Credit

Grave

If you have ever planned for a big life change, you have likely considered how much money you will need to make this change a reality. Anything can happen in your life and no matter how much you try to prepare for the unknown, you will realize that you will never have all the answers. The good news is that you don't need all the answers, just the right knowledge. Whether your life event is planned or if you simply want to be prepared for anything your future holds, you will need to become familiar with the terms "credit history" and "credit reports." These terms are not hard to understand, and you do not need to panic when you hear them.

By using proven strategies and having a clear understanding of what they both mean, you will be able to get a handle on both your credit history and your credit reports. Much like anything else, having knowledge about these both is like having power. You are going to feel like you have much more peace of mind when you understand exactly how your credit is affecting your life. When you make smart financial decisions now, you are giving your future a safety net. Knowing that you can become financially stable, even when you weren't previously, is a great feeling.

The following are some real-life examples that will illustrate the importance of your credit score and how it can affect you:

- For a new family, there are bound to be many life changes. From deciding to get married and then having your first child, life as a new couple is going to be full of decision-making and smart planning. To prepare for this expansion of your family, you will need to consider how you are going to buy a house of your own.

  For most, paying for a house in full is not a realistic option. The best way to purchase a home is by saving up for a healthy down payment and then financing the rest of the balance. You cannot do this at any time, especially when you do not have a good credit score. The banks are not going to want to loan you any money if they see that you are not in a financially stable place.

  By using your credit history to view your past transactions, the banks are going to be able to get a good idea of your spending habits. Through your credit report, they will understand how frequently you apply for and use credit and the ratio in which you are able to pay it back. Lenders are naturally going to want to give money to those who will be able to pay it back quickly. They do not care to take a risk on someone who potentially will not be able to make their payments.

- Imagine a different scenario now with someone who is middle-aged and has been working for most of his life. Put yourself in his shoes and picture going to a factory to work nearly every day for the last 30 years. Now, imagine that something unexpected happens, like a cancer diagnosis. This is a reality for many people, often very unexpectedly. Just when you thought you were about to reach the age of retirement; you are now suddenly being flooded with medical bills. Not only are you worrying about your health, but you are also worrying about any debt that you might leave behind for your family.

To better prepare for your future, you decide that you need to secure a life insurance policy. While making a couple of inquiries, it becomes apparent that the insurance companies are checking your credit. Through your credit report, they are able to determine your rates and the value of your plan based on your spending habits. Insurance is all about risk versus reward and most companies, much like lenders, are not willing to take on liability if they can help it. Without a decent credit score, you might be left with a minimal plan that only covers some of your expenses.

- The final scenario that you can picture is that of a divorced couple. After being together for decades, your relationship with your spouse has ended. Filing for divorce brings up the very scary reality that you now have to find a new place to live that is suitable for yourself and your three children. In an attempt to make ends meet, you consider what funds you have available. The joint bank account has been closed, leaving you with half of a small savings account that neither one of you tended to very much. Your only other option seems to revolve around relying on your four credit cards to keep you afloat.

After living in an apartment for a few months, you realize that the rent prices are very steep. In an effort to become more budget-friendly, you decide that you want to buy a new house. During this process, your credit report is going to be viewed and your credit history will be explored. Because your spouse was usually the one who applied for credit-related services, you realize that you have a low credit score on your own. Because you never took the time to build your credit, you are now left in a tough situation that requires you to build it in a hurry.

While these scenarios do not directly apply to your life, they can happen to anyone. The point is that your credit is the foundation to your ultimate financial stability. Whether you need to borrow money or find a new place to live, having a solid credit score is going to set you up for an easier experience. It is not a good feeling to realize that you cannot be considered trustworthy because of your credit score, so it is important that you work on improving it now before it is too late. Having a good credit score can help you build your reputation and highlight your spending patterns. In turn, you will be able to have access to all the things that you need.

Credit History

Laptop

To take the confusion out of improving your credit score, it is important that you understand exactly what your credit history is. You can think of it like an autobiography that tells a story about the kind of credit that you have applied for, how much credit you have used, and what kind of credit offers you have received. It will also show lenders if you pay your bills on time and if you have ever gone through any bankruptcies or liens. This is important for future lenders to know because it is going to shape how they view your reputation. If you have a bad credit history that shows you do not pay your bills on time, you will be unlikely to receive any more credit offers or, you will receive offers with high interest rates.

To break this down further, you should know exactly what the lenders would see so you have an idea of what kind of credit you qualify for. Keep in mind that they will be able to see all your current accounts, as well as accounts that have been closed. They will also be able to see how much you owe on each account. Your credit utilization, how much credit you have used, is another important factor in your credit history. If you have multiple credit cards, but you are only using a small percentage of your total credit, this is going to show that you can spend responsibly. Some people end up with bad credit scores because of high utilization percentages. An example of this would be if you had multiple credit cards, and they were all maxed out.

There is a section devoted to the payments you make. Lenders further look at your payment history to determine your financial responsibility. If you have a reputation for making 100% on-time payments, this is going to be great for your credit score. Any missed or late payments are naturally going to cause you to have a lower score. If you go for too long without paying a credit card, the amount owed can be sent to collections. This means you have missed your payment and ignored all warnings from your creditor. In this case, you would have to call the creditor to come to an agreement to settle your debt. This can take a negative toll on your credit score the longer you leave it unsettled.

Revolving vs. Installment

One of the final features on your credit report is that it tells lenders what types of accounts you have. There are two different types: revolving and installment. When you have a revolving credit account, there is no set amount in place. Most commonly, credit cards work as revolving credit. There is a limit in place for how much you are able to borrow, but your actual spending power within this limit is up to you. More often than not, revolving loans will be given in the form of credit lines. The creditor has control of the credit limit that is allowed, and they can usually increase it if they see that you are making on-time payments and using it to their liking.

Installment credit is different because you must pay it off in steady payments that are predetermined each month. When you are approved for the loan, you are given an amount. This amount will not change over time, regardless of your payment history. Because it is predetermined, it will end when you pay it off. Some examples of these include car loans and mortgages. While the amount will not change, you will usually have the option to refinance it after some time. If the interest rates aren't fixed, this means that they can go up, causing you to pay more. When you refinance, you might be able to get your payments and interest rate down which will allow you to pay it off sooner.

Each one of these types of credit will affect your credit score differently. When it comes to revolving credit, your payment history is going to be the factor that influences your score the most. Lenders recognize when you have a great payment history, so you should do everything that you can to make sure you pay your bills on time. If you are ever worried that you will not be able to make your payment, call your lender immediately. They will usually be able to work out a payment plan with you to accommodate you. If you call them ahead of time, this will also usually be enough to save your credit score from falling. Communication is important when it comes to having credit cards.

The next thing that will impact your score is how much credit you are using. As mentioned, credit utilization is important and just because you have it doesn't mean that you need to spend all of it. In general, your score can be expected to drop if you use over 30% of the credit that you are approved for. Anything below this is considered a financially responsible way to use credit. If you want a quick way to boost your score, getting your utilization down is one way to do this. With installment credit, this isn't such a big factor because the amount is fixed. They usually aren't even factored into your credit score because they are seen as an entirely different form of credit.

You can expect a more straightforward approach when it comes to the way that installment credit impacts your score. Your payment history is going to tell lenders everything they need to know. Making sure that you make your payments on time, much like with your other credit accounts, is going to put you in the best standing. The same rules apply — if you feel that you cannot pay your upcoming bill, reach out to your lender, and try to come up with some kind of payment plan that will not put you behind. As long as you are communicating correctly, you should have no problems with your payment history and the way it impacts your credit score.

How to See Your History

Your credit history is actually a part of your credit report. It is the main component. Normally, it costs money to see your credit history because you need to obtain your entire credit report. Legally, all consumers are allowed one free copy of their credit report each year from all three of the main credit bureaus. These are Experian, Equifax, and TransUnion. You can visit each of these companies' websites to obtain your free copies. Most people wonder why it is important to view a report that you have minimal ability to change. The main reason is that it is good to be aware of your financial standing. When you know exactly what is on your report, you will be able to see any problems that are preventing you from having better credit.

Maybe you need to get your credit score up to purchase a home. You wouldn't know where to begin if you had no idea what was on your credit report. Whether you need to balance out your credit utilization or get your payment ratio higher, your credit report is going to give you an idea of where to get started. When you are applying for certain jobs, you might need access to your credit report. Some employers will view this information as an indicator of whether you are qualified to work these jobs. These are known as background checks. Of course, landlords also check credit reports. They want to make sure they are renting to responsible tenants who are going to be able to pay them on time. When you think about it, a lot can revolve around this report.

Keep in mind that gaining access to your credit score too much can actually cause it to go down. It is important to know the difference between soft and hard inquiries. The former will not impact your credit score. Soft inquiries are the kind of inquiries that are commonly pulled. If you have ever wondered why you receive so many credit card offers in the mail, it is because these companies are able to run a soft inquiry, so they have an idea of how much spending power you have. You should be the only one who can see soft inquiries and they should be used for informational purposes.

Hard inquiries are run when you apply for a credit card or a loan. These will actually stay on your credit report for two years and any future potential lenders who view your credit history will see them. These are the inquiries that will lower your score by a few points. It is a common misconception that checking your score will lower it each time, but that is only true when a hard inquiry is being performed. This should not be a problem, as long as there are only a few hard inquiries made in a given period of time. If there are too many, this is going to show lenders you are on the high-risk side.

Credit Reports

Reports

You already know that your credit history makes up a part of your credit report, but what makes up the rest of it?

Your credit report is like your report card. This shows how and when you pay your bills, giving lenders an accurate picture of your financial responsibility. It will also show them how much debt you have and how long you have had each account. Some people go through periods of having minimal debt and then picking some up. Lenders like to know how you manage this debt because this gives them an idea of your spending habits. Sometimes, you will need to use credit for something important and then you will have to pay it off to keep your debt down. Other times, your debt might get away from you and cause you to spend years working to pay it off. No matter your situation, it is still possible to improve your report. Keep in mind that this is exactly why you are learning how to boost your credit score.

As mentioned earlier in the chapter, the three main credit bureaus are Experian, Equifax, and TransUnion. They are also known as Credit Reporting Agencies (CRAs). These companies are for-profit, and they are governed by the Fair Credit Reporting Act (FCRA). The main ways that these CRAs are able to obtain your information are through creditors such as your bank, credit card companies, and auto financers. They can also obtain information through your public records, which are easily accessible online, and they account for things such as property records and court records. Many people wonder why each CRA might have a different report for them and why even their credit score might differ. This is normal because some CRAs might pick up more information than others might. It becomes a smart idea to obtain all three reports, when possible, so you are able to see the full picture of your credit report.

When you apply for a loan or make a large purchase, your potential new lender could choose to look at one credit report or all three; that is up to their discretion. Much like you are able to see the bigger picture of your credit report, so will they. In viewing your reports, lenders will be able to determine how much of a risk you are. In other words, they want to know how likely it is that you are going to pay back the money that they loan you. This is an important factor for lenders because they don't want to take on any liabilities. Buying a house or a car can be incredibly difficult if you have low or no credit because your credit is what will represent you. When you apply to make a large purchase, or even to rent a place to live, you will typically have to give your consent to the lenders accessing your credit report and credit score. This is a common practice that should be expected.

Make sure you remember it is a *federal law* to be able to access your free annual copy of your credit report from each of the three CRAs. There are many ways that you can request yours, but the easiest way is by visiting AnnualCreditReport.com. If you prefer to request it over the phone, you can call 1-877-322-8228. If this is your first time requesting your report, you can set a reminder to request it again at the same time next year. Unless you plan to make a big purchase in the upcoming year, requesting it at the same time annually is going to give you a good idea if anything changes or if you should be aware of anything that stands out.

Most credit reports are going to look the same but knowing how to read one is important. The following is a breakdown of each section and what each entail:

Personal Information

This section is exactly as it sounds. Here you will find information like your name, address, and phone number. You will also see employment information if you are currently employed. While this is all basic information, having the report will benefit you because you will be able to spot any potential mistakes. If anything appears incorrect on your credit report, you will be able to handle it quickly before it impacts your credit score. People who do not check their credit reports will often go years without realizing that there are mistakes in it simply because they aren't paying attention to the smaller details.

Accounts

This section is also exactly how it sounds. Here, you will find all the credit accounts that are assigned to you. Everything from credit cards to mortgage loans will be found here. It is good to see this all on paper because you will be able to have an accurate idea of just how much money you owe and how well you are managing it. For some, viewing these reports can allow them to remember any debt that they might have forgotten about. If you have ever opened a credit card to make a single purchase, it can be easy to forget about since it is not something that you regularly use. By viewing your credit report, you will be able to see what is active and what you are responsible for.

Inquiries

All of your inquiries will be in this section for up to 25 months. You will be able to see the companies that have run the inquiries on your credit and when they did it. This can be another beneficial tool for you because you might spot something out of the ordinary. If you feel that your credit report was run by mistake, you can dispute this in an effort to protect your credit score. While it does not usually happen, it is possible. Because this information is accessible by so many companies, you need to make sure you recognize each one who is trying to check your credit score. Anything out of the ordinary should be disputed or at least brought up. This can save you a lot of time and hassle if there does seem to be an error.

Public Records

If you have ever experienced a large financial loss, such as a bankruptcy or civil judgment, this information would appear here. Many people do not have anything under their Public Records section, but it serves as another way for lenders to view what has been going on. This is the final section of your credit report and it helps to paint a full picture of your financial status. Most items on your Public Records will stay for seven to 10 years. Know that wrong information can be placed in this section by mistake, so reviewing it is important. If you see a bankruptcy listed under your name you know you did not file, this will greatly impact your credit score without you even realizing it.

Other than checking your credit report for informational purposes, there are certain times when you should request a copy. For example, if you were about to purchase a car or a house, it would be wise of you to access your credit report about three months in advance. This will give you plenty of time to review it and to dispute it, if necessary. As you look over the report, your goal should be to identify all the accounts and lenders that are listed. If there is anything that looks unfamiliar to you, it is worth looking into. This might be a red flag that allows you to save your credit score. If you are not going to be making any big purchases within the year, it helps to pick a date that you will associate with viewing your annual free credit report, as mentioned.

Some people like to do this on New Year's Eve because it is easy to remember, and it is the very beginning of the year.

Accessing your credit report is the first actionable step that you can take toward improving your credit score. Know that this information is going to give you more financial power and you will be able to think of more ways to improve your score when you understand exactly how to read this report. Remember, a credit report is not the same thing as a credit score. Your score is based on your credit report, but the two are not the same. If you want to find a way to make a large impact on the improvement of your score, you need to start from the source, which is your credit report.

Many people think paying extra on their credit cards will be enough to make a significant difference, but this isn't always the case. While this might boost your score by a few points, it is not going to make the biggest impact. Moreover, when your balance goes up again, this is only going to bring you right back to square one. To make a change that lasts, you need to create a plan for yourself that allows you to work on multiple areas of your finances to improve your score. Understand that there are many things you can do because you are in control of your spending power. By taking control of your credit score, you will see that this is not something that needs to cause you stress or confusion.

Chapter 2: The Good, the Bad, and the Ugly of How Your Score Is Calculated

Western

As you work on your credit score journey, you might be wondering where you fall on the scale. Is your score bad? Is your score good? There are many distinctions between the two, but at the end of the day, there is always going to be room for improvement. Even those with scores that are considered high can always benefit from taking more financial control over their lives and increasing their credit scores. Instead of focusing too much on the actual number, you need to consider if you are going to qualify to make the purchases and receive the loans that you need. You don't have to show a perfect score to finance your car, but you do need to prove that you are financially responsible and eligible to make such a purchase.

In this chapter, you are going to learn how your score is calculated and what range you fall into. Much like having a better understanding of your credit history and credit report, you are going to feel at ease when you understand what makes up your credit score. This also gives you the advantage of knowing how to boost it and how to remain within a range that makes you feel comfortable. Again, this should not be a stressful situation. Know that you are already taking steps to improve your score, so your focus should be kept on the end result. Worrying about it is not going to change it, so be easy on yourself. Many people end up becoming upset by their low score before they even make any plans to improve it. This journey is going to be different because you get to decide what happens next. You will get to take the steps that work best for your lifestyle.

Your Credit Score: A Full Picture

Frame

Thinking in simple terms, your credit score is a three-digit number. This number can hold a lot of power, though. It is meaningful because this number represents you in many different ways. By looking at your credit score, lenders are able to decide about whether you will be approved. While you might not want to apply for any loans or make any big purchases right now, there will come a point where you must do so. This is why your credit score is essential. You need to make sure you are doing everything that you can to boost your score so when you need to apply for these things, you will be approved. There is nothing worse than being declined because you neglected your credit score for all the years prior.

For some, working on your credit score is a regular part of your life. Maybe you have been working on it so much, yet you are frustrated to see minimal results. You might even feel panicked or stressed out because you feel that your score is never going to be in the "good" range. If so, you don't need to feel discouraged. The purpose of reading this guide is to learn about all the resources and tools that you will need to boost your score. A common misconception is that you will have a perfect score if you do not have any credit cards or loans. It actually works in the exact opposite way — no credit means that you will have a low score. When you have a few accounts that you can manage well, this is going to allow you to maintain a great score while still having a financial backup plan in place.

Your credit score can range anywhere from 300–825. When you don't have any credit, your score is going to be low; however, this is not the same thing as having "bad" credit. As soon as you open a line of credit and begin to pay it off, this is going to boost your score very quickly. Most people like to make a purchase that they know they can pay off right away just so they can establish some form of credit. When you are first starting out, it might be difficult to find a credit card company that is willing to take you on as a client. However, some companies offer introductory cards for first-time spenders that will allow you to open up a small line of credit.

Another option for first-time credit users is to be added as an authorized user. This means that you are added to an account that a family member or loved one already has in place. When you are given this authorization, you will be able to have your own card for the same account. All the activity that is recorded on their account will also appear on your account. You need to be careful if you decide to do this because you really need to trust the person who adds you as an authorized user. If you can find someone with a low balance who is notorious for making on-time payments, this can be a way to build or improve your existing credit.

You can also open what is known as a "secured card." This means that the card you apply for will require you to make an initial deposit.

By putting money down upfront, your credit line will be based upon this. When you only have a certain amount of money to spend, it won't be possible for you to forget to make payments. You will also definitely have all the money necessary to make the payments since you already put it down. With a couple of on-time payments under your belt, this can do a lot to build or improve your credit score.

The more that you spend while providing on-time payments, the more credit card companies will be willing to loan you. For example, after 30 days of responsible spending, your credit card might increase your limit by $500. It is common for this to happen, especially when you start out with a card that has a lower limit. This is a great way for you to start building your credit. However, keep in mind that you will have to pay back what you are spending. When you begin spending much more money than you actually have, this can lead to credit card debt and an increased interest rate. In turn, your credit score will go down, regardless of on-time payments. Remember, your credit utilization also matters.

According to a study by Experian, 99% of people have a credit score that is at least 470 or above. This includes those who are in a lot of debt and who cannot make on-time payments. It is rare to see your score drop any lower than this. According to a standard that is put in place by most creditors, a score of 700+ is considered "good." If your score is just below this, it does not necessarily mean that you will not be able to open lines of credit and obtain loans, though. Some companies are more lenient than others. If your score is only average, you might be given higher interest rates, but you will likely be able to get approved for the things you apply for.

Average, or fair, credit is considered between the 580–669 range. This means that 579 and below would be considered poor. No matter where your score is now, know that you can still improve it. Many people who have low to average credit are able to raise their scores into the "good" range easily. It takes a little self-discipline and keen attention to detail. For right now, if you have credit that is within the fair or poor range, you might not get the best offers from lenders you look into. Know that this will change, however, as soon as you are able to boost your credit score. You are still likely to find lenders that want to work with you, just know your options are going to be limited.

Thinking about your credit score on a smaller scale, imagine that you need to purchase a new cell phone or a satellite TV subscription. Your credit score is also going to be involved in this process. These companies check your score to determine your reliability. They want to know that you are going to be able to pay your bills on time. Depending on where your score falls, you might be required to pay a higher down payment if it is on the lower side. The same can be said when you are renting housing. Landlords, much like creditors, like to know that they are going to be paid consistently. They cannot afford to take on tenants who are going to become liabilities.

Now that you have a better understanding of why your credit score is so important, you can use this as motivation to make it even better. There are no tricks or gimmicks that will allow you to have a perfect credit score overnight. Time is definitely going to be a factor if you want to see an improvement. You need to allow enough time to pass so that your lenders can see your payment history and your usage. Most people become impatient during this process, but it is worth the wait. If you are able to create positive habits, they are going to continue to serve you and they will allow you to make sure that your credit stays within the “good” range where you want it to be.

What Influences Your Score?

Graph

This section is going to break down exactly what influences your credit score and how to control it. When you have an idea of what could potentially be lowering it, you will understand what needs to be done to improve it. Your credit score is never decided based on a single factor, so if you know that you have certain weaknesses, this does not mean that you will never have a high credit score.

Five different categories of information that comes from your credit report and influences your credit score. Each category holds a different "weight," or relevance. As you read about how your credit score is weighted, you will also be able to determine the things that will make it higher. This will give you a complete understanding of the scoring process.

1. **Payment History**: This has been discussed a lot, but it

remains one of the most vital aspects of your credit health. You can think of this as the most important factor that creditors look at. No matter how much money you borrow, it is essential that you are able to make your payments on time.

Few lenders are going to feel comfortable loaning you money, even if you insist that you can pay it off if you have missed or late payments on your credit report. This is why communicating with the credit card company or loan company is so important if you know that you aren't going to be able to make your payment.

When you can pay a little more than the minimum payment due, you are going to show your lender that you are financially responsible. By paying your card off early, even if you only have $5–$10 extra to add to your minimum balance, you are going to be lowering your interest as well.

Your payment history makes up for 35% of your entire credit score; that's close to half! It's one of the easiest things you can do. Make sure you are spending responsibly and set up payment reminders for yourself. If possible, you can place your card/loan payments on auto-draft, so you never have to worry about missing one.

1. **Amounts Owed**: Understandably, the amount of money that you owe to lenders is going to make up for a significant percentage of your credit score (30%). This category of information is also known as your utilization ratio. Along with tracking the amount of debt that you have, an evaluation of how much more you spend each month is going to be considered. With this information, creditors are going to get a good idea of your spending habits.

If you were not a responsible spender in the past, this information unfortunately will put you at risk of having a lower credit score. When your utilization ratio is too high, this is going to appear as a red flag to the lenders you approach. If you want to keep this number down to the recommended 30% utilization ratio, you should do your best to pay off, or make bigger payments on your high-balance credit cards.

Remember, the revolving credit is being looked at here. Your home loan and car loan will not be considered in this category because that is a loan at a fixed amount. Moreover, debt dissolves as soon as you pay it off. Because you can choose to spend as much or as little as you want of revolving credit, you must be more careful with these habits.

1. **Length of Credit History**: This category is something that you cannot change because it serves as an indication of how long each of your credit accounts has been open. This is another factor that you need to leave up to time. When you let your accounts mature, this shows creditors that you are able to have your accounts open for long periods of time while using them responsibly.

A common mistake that people make is paying off and closing out their lines of credit. When you do this, you are not allowing them the time to build up your credit history . It is better to keep the card active, even when you are not using it. This time is going to help improve your credit score, as it makes up for 15% of it.

If you do not have many mature accounts yet, you are just going to have to be patient. There is nothing that you can do to speed up this process. However, you can be informed on how much the length of your credit history actually impacts your score. If you have any children or loved ones who are younger, make sure you encourage them to open up their first small line of credit early on. This is going to give them an advantage by creating accounts that will have the chance to mature.

1. **Recent Activity**: Your recent activity is made up of three different categories. The first is how many credit accounts you have, both open and closed. The more you have, the more factors you will have to impact your credit score. Each of these accounts is going to have a different credit limit and a different minimum payment that is expected of you. Consider that the more accounts you have, the more payments you are going to have to juggle.

Also found in your recent activity are all of your credit inquiries that have appeared on your account. Remember, you can get different kinds of inquiries. Some come from applying for credit cards, while others come from renting a new home. This is going to impact your score if you have had a lot of hard inquiries on your account; these inquiries slightly lower your score.

The final category here is how many times you have applied for credit over the last 12 months. Whether you were approved or declined, this history will be found here. As a whole, your recent activity makes up for 10% of your credit score. It gives the CRAs a chance to see how much you intend on using credit for your purchases and how successful you are at using the accounts you do have.

1. **Credit Mix**: Based on the different types of credit you have, your credit mix shows the diversity of your accounts. It makes up for the final 10% of your credit score calculation. This means that each given category will list all your cards, mortgages, car loans, and other revolving credit.

While it is not necessary to have one of each of the above types of credit, having high lines of credit is going to show that you are financially responsible enough to have lenders trust you. Those who have credit cards, an auto loan, and a home loan are going to appear more experienced with credit than those who only have a single credit card.

Keep in mind that it is still about how you are able to handle your credit mix. Having a diverse portfolio isn't going to help you if you are unable to pay your bills or keep track of your payment dates. By keeping these factors in mind, you should be able to find a balance that fits your current lifestyle. In the future, you can always add more accounts to your credit mix as you need them.

FICO and VantageScore

FICO

You might be familiar with your Fair Isaac Corporation (FICO) score, as it is the most commonly used credit-scoring model since the time it was created in 1989. Ninety percent of lenders frequently use your FICO score as an indication of whether they should approve you. As discussed, it uses the data from your credit report to generate a credit score for you to use as a reference point. Your FICO score is going to be based on the exact example above. They are going to look at your payment history, amounts owed, length of credit history, recent activity, and credit mix to determine the score that you will receive. To obtain your FICO score, you do need to have at least one or more accounts that have been open for six months or longer. You also need to have at least one account that has been reported to a credit bureau within the past six months.

If you are new to earning credit, it is common for you not to have a FICO score until you meet the above criteria. Your information is gathered in a way that works in real-time. CRAs take a look at your credit during a specific point in time, therefore, explaining why you cannot have a FICO score unless you have had credit for at least six months. The data is specific to the time period that you check your score. This means that it can easily change the next time you check it because you could have opened a new account or paid off an old one. Anything is possible when the information is selected this way and examined in real-time.

Over the last few years, both scoring systems have evolved. Your FICO score will now generate two types of scores. The first is your base score, and the second is your industry-specific score. The base score is used to help predict your ability to pay off your debt based on your overall credit profile. This score will give you a number between 300 and 850. The industry-specific FICO score works a little differently. It helps to predict how likely you will be to pay off a specific type of debt. This might be an auto loan or a home loan. This score will usually be presented in the 250–900 range.

There are many ways for you to access your FICO score, with many credit card companies giving you the ability to view it regularly for free. Some sources will charge you money to obtain it, so make sure you understand all the terms and conditions involved with viewing your score. It can be easy to get caught up with the actual number of your score, but you can see that even the FICO score is able to provide you with two different options that range from two different scales. What is more important is how well you are handling each of the factors involved that make up your credit score. This is going to allow you to make a difference while working on raising it.

It can be beneficial to view your FICO score because it gives you a picture of what is going on with your credit right now. It can show you what lenders will probably see and allow you some insight as to why you may or may not be approved. If you need to apply for a large loan, it can prove to be beneficial to wait until you have some security with your credit score. Having a low FICO score means that it is low for the time being, but a lot can change, even within a month. Checking this score frequently, as long as it is free, can be helpful in allowing you to see that you are making some progress.

VantageScore

The VantageScore model was introduced in 2006. It was developed by the three main CRAs (Experian, Equifax, and TransUnion) to be used as a predictive scoring model that was meant to be easy to understand. Much like your FICO score, knowing your VantageScore will benefit you by giving you an idea of what lenders are going to see when you apply for more credit and as you are paying off your current accounts. Your VantageScore takes more factors into consideration when coming up with their numbers.

The more influential categories are your payment history (this is very important), the age and type of credit that you have, and how much of each credit limit is being used. Moderately influential are your total balances and debt. Falling the lowest on the list are your recent inquiries and your available credit. With all these factors combined, this is how VantageScore is able to give you a number. This model is typically able to provide a score to those who are new to building credit, or those who tend to be inactive with their credit. VantageScore is able to use the data that comes from one month of your credit history and with one account being reported in the past two years. This is why some people will have a VantageScore but not a FICO score.

Your VantageScore is predictive, meaning it is going to keep track of patterns that appear in your credit behavior. This information can consist of up to two years' worth of these habits to create an accurate picture of how you use your credit. Your VantageScore is only going to provide you with one type of score, as it does not provide an industry-specific version. When the VantageScore was first used, it ranged from 501–990. Now, it has been adjusted to 300-850 to match the FICO score. This allows you to compare the two accurately without having to adjust the calculation due to the range that they provide.

Accessibility is the same for your VantageScore as it is for your FICO score. You can usually access it through certain creditors or other personal finance websites. If you aren't careful, you might encounter certain websites that will make you pay to view your score. Know that there are going to be free sources and you shouldn't have a problem finding them to look at what your score currently is. By having both your FICO score and your VantageScore, you are going to be able to compare them while keeping in mind that they have different rating factors. It is also possible that the credit reports they access are going to have different information on them, therefore, resulting in a different score.

The numbers aren't meant to match up. They are meant to give you a general idea of where you stand, which is important when you begin staying on top of your credit journey. Because your scores fluctuate, especially your FICO score, don't feel discouraged if it isn't where you want it to be yet. This can easily change with a little self-discipline and some awareness. One of the main ways to make sure you do not damage your credit score is by lowering your spending . If you know that you do not have the money and you know that you will also not have it by the time your monthly bill is due, then a credit line is likely not going to be the best option for you. When you are smart with your money, your score is going to reflect this.

Chapter 3: Top Five Key Benefits of Having a Good Score

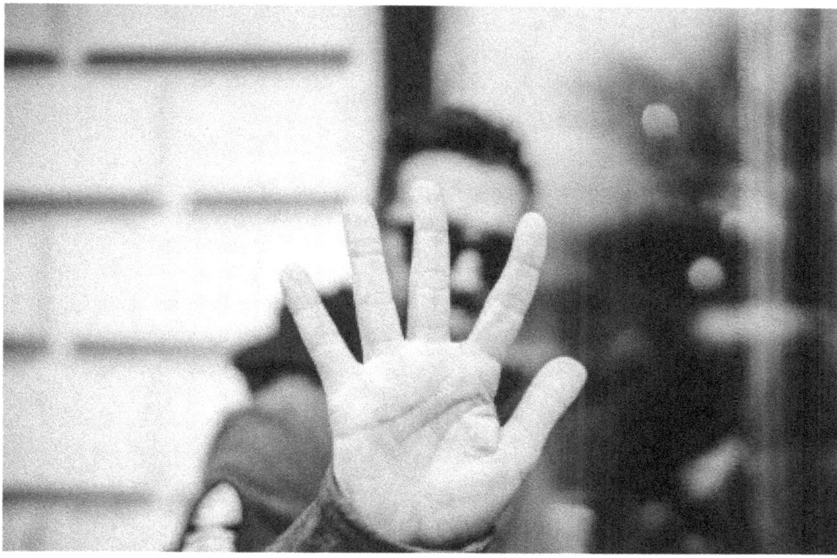

Five

Aside from the satisfaction that you will receive and a great reputation among creditors, there are other benefits to having a good credit score. When you have a good score, this is going to be recognized. Not only will you have more access to credit opportunities, but you are going to have better approval odds and lower interest rates. It becomes a luxury to know that you are going to be approved for any loan with a great interest rate to top it off. A lot of worrying stems from financial-related stress. When you can eliminate this stress, you are going to feel a lot more confident about being able to get what you need, when you need it.

Having good credit is a direct reflection of your hard work. There are no shortcuts or gimmicks, and if someone tells you otherwise, they are likely putting in extra work when they don't have to. As long as you stick to the principles that this guide provides, you are going to be well on your way to having a credit score that you can feel proud of. Below are some of the biggest benefits that you will experience when you commit to raising your credit score.

One: Lower Interest Rate

In general, the higher your credit score, the lower your interest rate will be. This is going to be helpful when it comes to paying off large balances. You might have enough money to cover the money that you owe, but it is often easy to forget about the interest rate. Many people borrow money and use credit without considering this factor . This is what can make paying off debt so difficult. When you apply for a credit card or another type of loan, you are given an interest rate in the form of a percentage. For a typical credit card, you can expect to pay 13%–25% in interest. This means that this percentage is going to be added to your balance each month that you spend paying it off. If it is not paid off quickly, this can definitely add up.

Some cards offer a 0% introductory interest rate. This sounds great, but make sure you read the fine print! Most credit card companies will offer you this, only to give you a high interest rate after the introductory period is over. It is important that you always read all the details that are involved before applying for any type of loan. If you are going to apply for a credit card or loan, make sure you do some comparative shopping. The offers might look equal at first, but their interest rates are going to define them. It would make sense to select a card with a lower interest rate because this is going to help you the longer you have a balance on the account.

When you work on your credit score, you will notice that some creditors are going to take notice of this and reward you by lowering your interest rates. This is going to be helpful when it comes to meeting your minimum payments and being able to pay off your debts quickly. Once you get the ball rolling on improving your credit score, this is going to make a difference in many other areas of your financial health. As you can see, everything is interconnected. For most, interest rates are going to be first experienced through applying for credit cards, so it is important that you have a good understanding of them before you apply for larger loans (home and auto).

Your credit score is considered when you apply for a mortgage loan. If you have a score in the good range, you can expect to pay an interest rate of around 2% in most cases. Because of how much money you are borrowing, this is going to help you pay it off quickly and efficiently. When you have a score that is closer to the 600 range, you can expect to be given an interest rate of around 4%. Imagine that your 20-year mortgage loan is $100,000. By the time the 20 years are up, you will have paid around $150,000 to the bank if you have a good credit score. If you have an average score, you will have paid close to $220,000. This is a staggering difference and a clear example of why retaining a good credit score is important.

There are some cases where you might need a personal loan to pay off your debt. Many people obtain personal loans, or consumer loans, to pay off their student loan debt. With this kind of loan, money is given to you in the sum of your debt and then you make a single monthly payment that is agreed upon when you are approved for the loan. Depending on how much you need, the bank is going to consider your credit score when it creates your interest rate. For most loans, you need to have a minimum credit score of around 680 if you want to be considered for approval in the first place.

When you have a higher credit score, your interest rate won't have as much of an impact on the amount that you owe. Some individuals who are badly in need of a loan will work with the first company that will accept them and their lower-end credit score. While they might get the approval for the loan, they are also getting an exceptionally high interest rate. Some of these personal loan interest rates can approach nearly 50% and this can add up incredibly quickly. Before you know it, you will be in debt just because you originally tried to get a loan to get out of debt. This type of snowball effect happens frequently, and it is the source of a lot of stress for many people.

If you do intend on applying for a loan, do your research and make sure you have an accurate idea of what your credit score is. Being quoted for high interest rates should tell you that now is not the right time to apply for a personal loan. It would be much more beneficial to keep paying off your debt and then waiting until you are able to raise your credit score to qualify for something better. By trading your debt off for more debt, nothing is going to change with your financial situation.

Two: Faster Loan Approval

When you do find a loan that you deem a good fit for your financial situation, you are going to be approved quicker when you have better credit. Your credit score is going to speak for you, showing the lender you make on-time payments and you know how to manage your loans. It is like applying for a job when you have years of experience versus months of experience. The better your credit score, the more valuable experience you will have with managing your debt. Lenders love to see responsibly used credit with a great rate of utilization.

In case of an emergency in which you would need to obtain a loan quickly, it helps to have this extra security in knowing that you are going to be approved. If your credit score is around 700 or higher, this usually results in an automatic approval. Depending on how high it is, you will also receive certain benefits, like a lower interest rate. If your score is around 570 or under, you can expect to receive an automatic rejection. Remember, a score this low can be an indication that your credit needs fixing, but it can also indicate that you are just starting out. Either way, lenders want to see experience, so they are going to pass until you can prove that you have enough of it.

You might not be concerned with being approved for a loan now, as plenty of people are not, but you need to consider your future. If you ever plan to buy a house or a new car, you are likely not going to be able to pay for either one upfront. You never know when you might need to move, whether you outgrow your old home because you are starting a family, or if your rent is not fixed and your landlord keeps raising it. Life is full of unpredictable occurrences and it makes sense to be prepared for them rather than assuming they will never happen to you.

If you are convinced that you aren't going to buy a car in the next few years, consider if something were to happen to the one you are driving now. This car usually takes you to work and to all the errands that you need to run on a weekly basis. Mobility is important for most people and you are likely included. There are other ways to get around, but the convenience of having your own ride is one that you cannot beat. While most people believe they will be able to buy a new car if something happens to their old one, having enough money isn't always going to be a guarantee that you will be approved for the car loan. If you have the money, but you have a bad credit score, you might not be approved for the loan at all. This would put you in a difficult situation and you would likely have to settle for a cheaper car to get something situated.

There are many real-life examples that you can put into context for yourself just by imagining the what-ifs. It is important to prepare for anything by staying ahead of your finances. Being able to obtain a loan if you need one is like having a backup plan. You never know where your life is going to take you, so you might as well prepare for these moments. If you want to get married and you want to have a wedding, for example, this can be expensive. Of course, you don't want to deny yourself of this special celebration. Your good credit score can be exactly what you need to make your dream a reality.

Three: Higher Credit Limit

Credit Card

With a higher credit limit, this means you will be able to borrow more money. For most with lower credit scores, you are either going to be declined when you apply for a credit card or you are going to be provided with a low limit. Some cards will only start out with $300–$500 limits until you can raise your credit score and show them that you are able to handle a higher limit. What you do at the beginning of your credit journey is going to shape the rest of it greatly. For example, if you have a lower credit score and you are approved for a $500 credit card, your score is going to get even lower if you max this card out and miss your payments. This is only going to show the creditors that you are not able to use it responsibly.

A common mistake that is made is getting too comfortable with your newfound spending power. It is easy to get carried away with using your credit card, even if you don't have the money to pay it back right away. It becomes a good practice to make sure you have at least most of the funds you are spending, or else you are going to end up in a lot of debt and several months, even years, of paying it back. The average American household has around $5,700 worth of debt. This shows that having a credit card, or credit cards, can be too much for some people to handle. If you have allowed your spending to get out of control, you do not have to feel ashamed. By committing to boosting your credit score, you are also going to be simultaneously lowering your debt.

Another thing to consider about having a higher credit limit is what this is going to do for your credit utilization rate. If you have a credit limit of $1,000 and you have spent $500, this is going to put you at a 50% utilization rate. Now, imagine that you have been making your payments on time and you are paying more than the minimum amount due each month. Because of this, your credit score rises, and your creditor decides to increase your credit limit to $1,500. This will automatically bring your credit utilization rate down to 33% without having to change anything that you are doing, and this is all because you were able to boost your credit score. As you know, being around 30% credit utilization or lower is considered ideal.

This factor might not have mattered to you in the past, but you can see how important it actually is. Your credit limit is going to dictate a lot about how you are able to spend. Whether you are building your credit for the first time or working on boosting your current score, you need to remember that your credit card should be treated like emergency money. If you get into the habit of using it daily, it is going to run out before you know it and you might not have a way to pay it back. Think about your credit card as money that you do not have until you need to use it in a pinch. It will serve as a solid backup plan that you will easily be able to pay off without getting yourself into any major debt.

Not every credit card is going to start you out with the same credit limit. Some cards will not accept you until you have a high enough credit score, while others are designed for those with lower scores. With all the benefits that come along with each card, it is a wise idea to apply carefully, as you would with a loan or any other type of lender. You might be able to benefit from things such as cashback or discounts on certain goods and services. You definitely should not feel like you have to settle for the first credit card that you qualify for because there might be better ones out there for you. Remember, a high credit limit does not necessarily equate to a better one. You also need to read the fine print and consider the interest rate.

Those who are financially responsible might have several credit cards, yet their utilization rate is likely going to be low. You should aim for this goal if you already have plenty of credit accounts that are open. If you are just starting out, you can have a few credit cards, but there is no need to overdo it. If you end up juggling too many cards, this is only going to result in a payment schedule that will probably be difficult for you to manage and successfully pay off. In addition, you are going to see this impact your credit score negatively.

Four: Lower Bills

If you commit to boosting your credit score, you might be rewarded with the possibility of lower monthly payments on your other bills! This is a great benefit and motivational factor of keeping your credit score in a good range because it can make many other aspects of your life easier. Because several service providers view your credit report and your credit score, they are going to take notice when they see that you have a high score and an excellent financial reputation. Service providers are willing to give you this benefit because you have proven that you have an excellent track record when it comes to paying off your debts. It is going to give them peace of mind to know that you are also going to be a great customer for them.

Insurance companies tend to consider your credit score frequently. If you have medical insurance or life insurance, you might be offered lower monthly premiums based on your score. Even if you have medical-related debt, the insurance companies take into consideration how well you are doing with paying it off and how quickly you are lowering this debt. They want to see that you are making a big effort at paying off your debt. Those who can only make minimum payments are going to take a lot longer to live debt-free. They will also not be likely to increase their credit score by much in the process.

If you have recently moved and opened a new account with a utility company, they are likely to look at your credit score. Imagine being able to get a discount on your utility bill simply because you can prove that you are on top of paying your other bills. This is essentially what happens when you can show them you have a good credit score. These companies like to know that you are going to pay your bills on time to prevent utility shut-offs. It causes the company an inconvenience when they must constantly suspend your account and reopen it. If you have ever had any past utility companies, your current one is definitely going to look into your history. They want to make sure they are taking on a reputable customer.

Almost everyone that you know has a cell phone. It is the easiest way to stay connected and to remain a part of the conversation wherever you are. Some cell phone companies recognize the hard work that comes with achieving a high credit score. They are willing to lower plan rates for those who have proven they are responsible with their funds because they see these individuals as assets. Much like utilities, your phone service will also be switched off when you cannot pay your bill. This involves the phone company turning it off and then reactivating it when you are able to pay your balance. Imaginably, cell phone companies prefer those with an excellent track record of making on-time payments. They want to see paid bills in a timely fashion, much like any other service provider. If you cannot prove that you are able to do this, some companies might turn you away or require you to join a plan with someone else who is more reputable.

Your high credit score is going to help you in this regard by saving you money. At the end of the day, the discounts that you receive that are based on your credit will put additional money back into the bank. This can be turned into savings for your family or money that you can put toward a renovation project. The possibilities are endless when you have a little extra money to spare because it adds up very quickly. It can be hard to save money, especially when you feel that you are only making ends meet. This is why working on your credit score is an actionable step you can take. By having an awareness of your spending habits, you can prevent yourself from falling even further into debt, giving you a better chance of paying off what you currently owe.

Most who do not pay attention to their credit scores believe that there is little that will change if they raise this number. Even a 10-point increase can amount to plenty of benefits, as you can see. If you are only able to make small steps right now, this is what is going to amount to bigger steps in the future — everyone must start somewhere. If you are tired of feeling like you are working only to give your entire paycheck to the bills you owe, start working on your credit score and see what this can change for you.

Five: Better Rental Property

When you first move to a new city, you are likely going to have to start out with a modest apartment that is good enough to provide you with the basics. Any time that you move somewhere new, you are going to need to adjust your bearings and make sure that your income is going to support you successfully so you can continue to live there. Most people start out with a co-signer unless they are able to provide a higher down payment and prove they have a good past rental history. This is why references are typically required. Landlords would much rather fill their apartments with individuals who are supported by the certainty that rent is going to be paid on time. This is why co-signers are so popular for those who are first-time renters.

A lot of trust must be placed on you when you find someone who is willing to cosign because it is the co-signer's credit on the line. If you fail to pay your rent, their credit score is going to suffer. For this reason, most people are only able to obtain a co-signer for a short period of time. After this, they must build up their own credit score to be able to rent a property on their own. While this provides a nice sense of independence, it also comes with a lot of hard work attached. You know that boosting a credit score does not happen overnight, so the process can feel endless.

If you have a fair credit score, you might qualify for a handful of apartments or homes to rent. While they might be places that you can see yourself living, it is up to the landlord to decide if your credit score is good enough to be approved. Because this is up to their discretion, you cannot exactly guarantee that you are going to get the apartment you want if your score is only average. This is a step in the right direction, though, because everyone must start from somewhere.

Good credit is going to stand out. It is going to tell landlords you are very qualified to rent their property, and this is simultaneously going to give you access to more places where you can live. When you have more options, this is going to give you more freedom. Moreover, your down payment might even be lower in the same way that service providers will give you a discount for having a good credit score. When you don't have to come up with as large of a down payment, you will likely be able to move in sooner and settle into your brand new place.

Those with bad credit scores tend to struggle because they feel that their options are limited. They must sometimes choose to live in unfavorable areas just because that is the only area where they will be able to find landlords that will approve their applications. If they find a decent neighborhood, they might still have to make sacrifices because they might have to go with a smaller space or one with fewer benefits because of the price range. With a high down payment being asked, this leaves little room for additional money that can be spent on a rental with more benefits.

If you want to continue working your way toward better rental properties and eventually, a place of your own that you do not have to rent, it makes sense to prioritize your credit journey. Make sure you are taking every step you can to increase your score and to keep it high. It can fluctuate so easily; one wrong move and you will be drowning in debt. You must always remember to live within your means, but keep your eyes set on your goals because you can make them happen when you are committed to improving your credit score.

There is no worse feeling than getting denied for a place that you could truly see yourself living. Don't let these declinations discourage you. Instead, you can take action and make the necessary improvements to your financial habits that will make positive impacts on your credit score. The next time that you feel you are never going to find a rental property within your range, make sure you take an actionable step. Make a double payment on one of your credit cards or save money that you would normally spend on credit. With a few of these small steps, you will slowly begin to see your score rise and you will soon be able to experience all the great benefits that come along with it.

Chapter 4: Top 10 Myths that Prevent You from Having a Good Credit Score

Do Not Enter

A lot of misinformation is spread about your credit score on a regular basis. Much like anything else, if you are used to hearing it repeatedly, it is more likely that you will believe it is true. This chapter aims to debunk some of the most common misconceptions that revolve around your credit score, giving you better knowledge to boost your score and see your highest credit potential. The next time that you hear information that discourages you and leads you to believe that you cannot improve your score, consider these myths and how there are always workable solutions for nearly every financial situation that you find yourself in.

The good thing about credit is that it is made to be temporary. Whether you are using a credit card or paying off the mortgage on your home, these debts are only meant to get you from point A to point B. Ideally, you should be able to pay them off and live a life that is debt-free if you make smart choices. For some, debt is inevitable based on certain expenses and life circumstances, but that still doesn't mean that it is permanent. Once you explore some of these myths, you are going to have a better understanding of which ones apply to you and how they have shaped your view on your credit score for all these years.

You'd be surprised to know how many people learn false information that prevents them from improving their scores simply because they do not think it is possible. According to a survey by NerdWallet in 2017, 2,000 Americans were asked what they knew about bad credit and how it can impact their lives. The results revealed the following:

- Forty-nine percent of Americans did not know that there was a correlation between their credit scores and their cell phone providers.
- Twenty-three percent believed that everyone could only have one credit score.
- Forty-one percent thought carrying a small balance on a credit card each month would help to improve their credit scores.
- Twenty-one percent believed that having a credit score of at least 600 would guarantee approval for any credit card that you apply for.

With the given rates of people being uninformed or misinformed, it is clear that there is some sort of disconnect between how your credit score works and how you can actually impact it positively. As you read each of the myths, take note of how many you have heard throughout your life. It is possible that even your parents believed these same myths, therefore, passing them down to you. A lot has changed in the world of credit and finance, in general, so it is important that you stay up to date.

1. **Debt Is All the Same**

Not all debts are equal, and this is important to keep in mind because your debt is likely going to come from different sources. Having a $150,000 debt can mean two things, depending on its source. If you have this debt because you maxed out five credit cards to pay for your wedding, this is going to put you in a tough spot. Not only will you have five different payments to manage, but you are also going to have five different interest rates to deal with. By only being able to pay the minimum due on each card, it is going to take you years to pay this debt off.

Now, consider that your $150,000 debt comes from the home that you have recently purchased. In this case, you fall in line with many other Americans who have mortgages. Because these debts are not revolving, you know that they will go away as soon as you are done paying them off. In addition, there are refinancing options available as you go. If you have a great payment history, you might qualify for a home refinance that will lower your monthly payments. When you refinance, the lender considers your entire loan, adjusting it if you qualify for a reduction. This can help you tremendously because it will allow you to pay off your large debt sooner.

You need to make sure you are comparing apples to apples when it comes to debt. Oftentimes, people will give themselves permission to run up their credit card balances because they believe that they are not the only ones in hundreds of thousands of dollars' worth of debt. While this is true, it is an unfair comparison when the debt is not going to reflect in the same way on your credit report. Any incredibly high credit card balance is bound to backfire on you because the interest is going to catch up to you. When the interest is added on, you are going to pay significantly more than you originally intended. You are also going to be stuck in a cycle of being responsible for this debt for a long time. If you have already reached a situation like this, you need to take your card out of your wallet and do your best to stop reaching for it until you are more financially secure.

1. Paying off Debt Instantly Maximizes Your Score

If you have the option to either pay off your debt in a lump sum or through regular monthly payments, you might feel like it is an easy decision to pay it all off at once for the sake of your credit score. This is actually not going to help you as much as you think it will. While your debt is going to be gone, so is your credit utilization. Remember, creditors like to see that you *are* using your credit limit. When you have nothing owed, you will mess up your credit utilization rate. In turn, this might prevent future lenders from approving you because they see that you are not using the credit that you were given.

Alternatively, if you decide that you want to pay off your debt with larger payments than the minimum due, make sure this is money that you have to spend. Some people will apply for a personal loan to pay off their bills. Not only is this hurting your credit score, but it is also putting you in more debt. It is better to pay what you can, as long as you are meeting your minimum payment deadlines. This consistency is going to boost your credit score much more than paying off your balance with a borrowed lump sum.

Be careful with refinancing, as well. A refinance is meant to lower your debt while making it easier for you to make monthly payments. If you repeatedly apply for refinancing options, this is going to create many inquiries on your credit. Regardless of if you are approved, your credit score will likely suffer in the process. This is why many experts recommend making your usual monthly payments as the best solution for boosting your credit score. If you can make larger payments while still staying financially on track, feel free to make them.

1. Closing Accounts Will Increase Your Score

Once you have already opened multiple accounts, closing them is not the same thing as never having them. In fact, it has been known that closing your accounts can actually damage your credit score. If you pay off your accounts and you do not want to use them, simply use your self-discipline to ensure that you do not run up a high balance again. It can be tempting to try to close out the accounts you have paid off, but you never know when you might need to use one as a financial backup plan.

While creditors do look at how much credit you have available, this is not what directly impacts your credit score. You can have $300,000 of available credit, but the amount that matters is how much you are actively using. When your credit is unused, it isn't going to count negatively against you. It is okay to let your accounts remain there until you decide to use them again. Even if you never use them again, it is still okay to let them remain as they are.

Consider that closing an account is going to impact your overall credit utilization rate. If you close an account that provided you with a $5,000 credit limit, this is going to increase your utilization rate significantly if you have balances on other cards. Because this amount will no longer make up the portion of available credit, it is going to appear that you have more utilization than you used to. Being smart about this decision can save you from causing an unnecessary spike.

The good thing about debunking this myth is that you will realize that no action needs to be taken if you find yourself with an account that has no balance. Simply continue to spend your money responsibly and make sure you are making your payments on time — that's it! This simplifies the misconception that you need to keep your accounts down to a minimum amount.

1. When You Have a Great Job, You Will Have a Great Score

Regardless of the job you have, this is not going to impact the strength of your credit score. Many are under the misconception that if you have a high-paying job with a high-ranking status, you are going to have a better credit score. This actually has nothing to do with your score, nor will it influence it. If you were thinking about getting a "better" job to improve your credit score, know that it isn't going to make a difference if you work as an office executive or as an entry-level associate.

As it has been explained, your credit score is going to revolve around the same factors, no matter who you are. These include your payment history, your utilization rate, and the length of time that your accounts have been opened. By taking away the association that your credit score is in any way related to the job you have, this is going to take away some unnecessary stress that you might have been holding onto.

One of the few ways that your job would make a difference to your credit health is if you were paid a higher salary, giving you the option of paying off your accounts sooner. Alternatively, earning more money will allow you to put more money into savings. If you ever needed to make an unexpected purchase, you will have this money available to you immediately rather than using a credit card. As long as you are meeting all of your financial obligations, then your score is going to reflect this.

1. Frequently Applying for Loans Will Boost Your Score

This is a myth because it is based on an idea that is actually true. If you have different loans from a variety of sources (home mortgage, auto loan, etc...), you are going to boost your score as long as you are paying them off and using them responsibly. Each time that you apply for a loan, however, you need to keep in mind that the lender is going to do a hard inquiry. With every hard inquiry done, this is going to lower your credit score by a couple of points. Eventually, this will be worth it to get the loan approvals, but it shouldn't be done unnecessarily.

This myth is based on the practice known as "loan shopping." With most other things, shopping is a great thing to do, but you should not live by this principle if you need a loan. Do your research and read about all the terms and conditions before you apply. When you finally apply, you are making a commitment to this loan and to having a hard inquiry done. This is one way that you can be smart about borrowing money when it is necessary for you to do so.

1. When You Have No Debt, You'll Have the Best Score

Having no debt is not equal to having a credit score of 800. It is considered negative to have no debt because this equates to having no experience with credit. While you can try to get creditors to take your word for your ability to pay on time, they are not going to believe this until they are able to see a record of it on paper. When you have a way to prove that you are financially responsible, your credit score will be able to speak for you.

So many people are under the wrong impression that they should hold off on opening a credit account for as long as possible. In a myth that was debunked prior, you already know that your score isn't going to be zero, anyway. It is likely going to be in the 300 range, and it takes the use of credit to build this up. If you have been hesitant to open up an account, take this as your sign to do so now. The sooner you get started, the more history you will have to show creditors.

When a creditor is not willing to lend you money because of a low score, even when you have never had a bad credit experience in the past, this can feel like a huge rejection.

Instead of trying countless creditors to see if they will approve your application, you can use some techniques that were already mentioned for getting started, like becoming an authorized user on someone's account or applying for a card that has a low limit. Many store-related credit cards tend to provide lower limits and more accessibility so that more people sign up and shop there.

1. If You Have More Savings and Debts, Your Score Will be Higher

The amount of money that you have in your savings account is not connected to your credit score. If you are well off, yet you cannot remember to pay your credit card bills on time, this is going to impact your score. Many people believe that if they have more money saved up, creditors will deem them more trustworthy because it will appear that they can pay off their debts easily. This isn't true because creditors are not going to be looking at this information.

Your bank balance can change every single day. You never know how much you are going to need to spend, so your savings account can fluctuate. This is why creditors cannot successfully gauge someone's financial responsibility by how much money they have. This is the same principle behind why creditors do not care what you do for a living or where you work. None of this information is actually relevant to your ability to pay your bills. It also does not prove that you have experience with successfully managing credit that you are approved for.

The same can be said for the misconception that you need to have a high amount of debt if you want to maintain a high credit score. Everything involves balance. If your debt is too high, you are going to struggle while paying it off. You need it to be enough that you can manage, but not non-existent, either. Starting slow is the best way to figure out your limit. You can always add debt to your life, but it becomes a lot harder to take it away once it is already there.

If you have ever felt the pressure to invest for the purpose of your credit score, you don't have to worry about this, either. Your investments are treated the same way as your savings — they will not automatically qualify you for a great credit score. Investing can be a great thing to do when you feel confident in your ability to manage your money and watch it grow, but it is not going to benefit the health of your credit.

1. It Takes Time to Ruin Your Credit Score

You likely know someone who is in more credit card debt than you are. Surely, you think, it will take a long time for you to rack up tens of thousands of dollars' worth of debt like them — this is incorrect. It is just as easy to create debt as it is to spend money. In fact, spending too much money is the number one way that people usually accumulate debt. It doesn't take much time at all before the CRAs are given this updated information, readjusting your score, as necessary.

It can happen very quickly because CRAs are always in contact with your creditors and other lenders. If you suddenly rack up a higher balance, you can expect to see this reflected in your credit score within the next month or so. After this happens to you, it can take months, or even years, to repair your score and get it back to what it used to be.

Even if you aren't spending too much of your credit limit, you can ruin your score in other ways.

Missing your first payment might not ruin your score, as many creditors are willing to work with you if you have never been late before. If you turn this into a habit you will quickly see your score lower before your eyes. As you know, your payment history is a crucial part of what makes up your credit score. Even if you only slip-up a few times, this is going to reflect poorly on your credit report. Those who have made mistakes like these have seen their score drop 100+ points in a short amount of time. This can be a devastating repercussion from something that could have easily been avoided.

You can never be so certain that you will be able to reverse these mistakes because they take a much longer time to correct. Creditors will make you earn their trust back, having to prove your financial responsibility in a consistent way before your score will start to go up again. Getting back on track can feel like a huge chore, but it is important to know that it is possible for you to do this. Patience is required if you want to see real results.

1. Getting Married Improves Your Credit Score

When you are married, you do qualify for some financial benefits in life. Your insurance is discounted, you will be able to obtain social security benefits, and you can even file your income taxes in a more streamlined way. One thing that marriage does not change, however, is your credit score. Because being married gives you plenty of other advantages, many people mistakenly believe that it will also impact your credit score. This isn't true, though.

To break this down further, if you have a joint credit card with your spouse, you must keep in mind that this *can* impact your score if one of you uses the card irresponsibly. The same rules apply when it comes to maintaining a great score, but the fact that you are married in itself is not enough to give you a better or worse credit score. Creditors are not allowed to consider your personal information. This means that they cannot base your score on who you are dating or how long you have been together.

Following the same principle, your credit score will not decrease if you are divorced or separated. Because your score has always revolved around factors that do not involve your personal life, you do not have to worry about damaging it in the process. The only time another person can impact your credit score is if you are an authorized user on an account with them. Alternatively, if you have co-signed for someone, this can also impact your score.

1. Having a Low Score Makes You a Bad Person

One of the hardest things to remember is that who you are as a person is not directly related to your credit score. It becomes so easy to punish yourself for having a low score, but this is not a reflection of your wonderful qualities. The decision that CRAs make while assigning your scores has nothing to do with your life decisions or your personal choices. The only thing that your score dictates is how big of a risk it would be for creditors to loan you money. Based on this number, it is up to their discretion whether they'd like to take on the risk.

Even the greatest, most honest people can have low credit scores. Maybe they missed a few payments or accidentally ran up a high balance that is now unmanageable. Because of how quickly you can damage your score, this is not something you can blame on your personality or traits. The same can be said about people who are terrible in their personal lives and with their choices — they might have earned great scores because they are consistent with their payments and have self-discipline when it comes to their credit usage.

When you can take away the stigma that comes with having a bad credit score, you are going to feel a lot better about yourself and a lot more confident in your ability to get it back up. This is never a reflection of your character that you should use against yourself. Sometimes, your score is going to drop, but you now have the knowledge that it takes to get it back up and feel great about it in the process. As long as you are making it a point to pay your bills in a timely fashion, reduce your balances to the best of your ability, and only apply for more credit when you need it, you are going to focus your habits in a way that will reflect positively on your score.

Awareness

Now that you are aware of some myths that are still circulating when it comes to your credit score, you should feel more informed about what it takes to lower your score. Being aware of your spending habits and how they impact your life is one of the biggest signs of financial responsibility. If you are the kind of person who checks your statements regularly, this is a sign that you are going to have the necessary observational skills to stay on top of your credit spending. Make sure that you recognize your charges and that the creditor is adhering to the credit limit and interest rate provided.

The instant you see anything that does not make sense or that you have no recollection of, call the creditor to get more details. This paired with your responsible payment schedule and spending habits, will keep you on track of your credit journey. Once you get into the habit of being this observant, it is unlikely that you will fall victim to any of the myths that used to deter you in the past. By staying informed, you will also be able to help others in your life stay informed. When it comes to your credit score, having accurate and up-to-date information is the key.

It is likely that you have been living by some of these myths, as have so many other people that are trying to boost their credit scores. This information continues to circulate because many people think understanding your credit score is a complex chore. Having this knowledge is not complex, nor should it be a chore. This information is going to guide you and you can think of it as a way to debunk all the myths that will likely continue to circulate. By taking back the control over your financial health, you are going to feel empowered, not overwhelmed.

Chapter 5: Maximize Your Score

Trophy

In this chapter, you are going to learn about the different ways you can maximize your credit score. After learning about how your credit score is calculated and how your credit report and credit history impacts your score, you should have a solid understanding of what this is going to entail. These tips are meant to help you take action now and not allow yourself to feel that you are stuck without options. Your credit score should not rule over your life, even though it can play a very important role. You are going to learn how to work with your score, making choices that are going to boost it and put you in better financial standing with creditors.

These tips are not meant to make a temporary impact on your credit score. They are real solutions that you can apply to your life right away. The sooner you get started with turning them into habits, the more natural they will feel. When working on boosting your score, know that you do not have to aim for a perfect one, as this is a difficult goal to obtain. Make your goal realistic and you will not be disappointed in yourself because you will be able to reach it. Remind yourself that it takes little steps to make the bigger picture work for you. With a little hard work and determination, you are going to see a credit score that reflects all your newfound habits.

Do your best to leave the comparisons at the door. Your financial situation is unique, and it should not be compared to anyone else's. Just because your friends only have one credit card each and high credit scores does not mean that you will automatically follow suit. Life brings up endless possibilities. Therefore, you might unexpectedly have to spend money on credit or apply for a loan. That is why the options exist — so you can have a backup plan. A lot of your stress will be removed once you realize that no one is living under the exact same circumstances as you.

The best part about your credit score is that you do not have to share it with your friends, family, or other loved ones. This information is as private as how much money you keep in your bank account. It does not need to be shared unless you want it to be known. You have the ability to keep it private and silently work on your goals until you are happy with the number that you see. This is another way to take the pressure off yourself and realize that this journey is meant to serve you, not anyone else. It is something that represents your own individual financial standing.

As you work through these steps, you might feel like you are already doing some of them. If so, that's great! Continue to do them and your consistency will pay off. Many people start out with great habits, but they can easily get off track because they become forgetful or they just don't feel like they are making a big difference. The little things that add up, creating a higher score that you can feel secure about. If it helps, you can keep these tips where you can see them as a reminder for what you are striving for. When you make something a regular part of your daily routine, you are less likely to stop doing it.

How to Take Action

Fast Car

- **Regularly Review Your Credit Report**: The first step is simple because all you need to do is read. Now that you are familiar with the ins and outs of your credit report, you can expect to know what you should see on it. By regularly reading and reviewing your report, you are going to be more likely to spot any inconsistencies or suspicious spending habits. These things will appear as red flags, the more familiar you become with your credit report.

Since you do not have to spend any money to read your report, all you must remember to do is obtain your free annual copy from each of the three CRAs. As mentioned in an earlier chapter, you can remind yourself to do this at the beginning of the year or a few months before you are supposed to make a big purchase. This kind of consistency is going to lead to a great habit.

If you ever have questions about something that you see on your credit report, don't be afraid to contact your creditors and ask them. It is better to be well-informed than to not understand something that is directly impacting your credit score. Since you have three different sources to get your credit report from, comparing them can be important because all three CRAs might pull different information to compile into your report.

What you see on one report is not necessarily going to be reflected in the other two. It can be interesting to see which CRAs pull which information. It is okay if the reports do not match, as long as all the information being reported is accurate and true to date. You might notice some information on your credit report that once was true but might no longer be accurate. This would be another reason to dispute your credit report or to contact your creditor for more details on the item that you are concerned about.

You do not need to become obsessed with viewing your credit report, especially since it isn't going to change much unless you move, open a new account, or spend a significant amount of money. Your credit report is something that you cannot change unless you dispute it, so there is no need to get wrapped up with it unless you need to make changes. A yearly viewing is fine with the occasional additional view if you have a big purchase to make in your future. By deciding when you are going to review your report, you are regaining control over the situation. It will no longer cause you stress because you will know exactly when to view it, how to obtain it, and what it all means.

You can keep your annual credit reports on file for an easy year-by-year comparison. It can help to motivate you when you can see the progress that you are making each year. You'll notice when balances fluctuate and when you are approved for new accounts. Sometimes, all it takes is a bit of tangible progress to keep going until you reach your next goal. If you ever encounter a source that asks you for money to view your credit report, you do not have to obtain it from this source. As long as you have not yet redeemed your free copy of your report, you can go directly to Experian, Equifax, and TransUnion to read them.

- **Review Your Credit Scores**: You likely have many ways to look at your credit scores without even realizing it. In the past, it used to be a lot harder for consumers to know where to begin, but in recent years, the process is actually easier than ever. Starting with your bank, look at their homepage or mobile app because there will usually be a link that allows you to view your updated credit score. This service is almost always going to be free with any financial institution that you use nowadays. Banks want you to be able to access this information so you can make smart and informed decisions.

Each of your credit card companies might also provide you a way to view your scores. In the same way that you would check it from your bank, you can visit the creditor's websites or mobile apps to see if they allow you to view them. Credit tracking is something that many people are becoming more aware of, and creditors can see this. They want to make it simple for their customers and, in turn, will make their customers even more responsible when it comes to making on time payments and using their credit wisely.

If you have not already gone to the three CRAs to obtain your credit scores, you can use services such as Credit Karma that will do this on your behalf. This will not lower your score because they are technically asking for this information in place of you, so you will only be given a soft inquiry. People enjoy using services like Credit Karma because they can make it a one-stop process to view their scores. In addition, these services might offer advice or other helpful resources for those who are looking to boost their scores. As they are not charging you to view your score initially, you might have to pay a fee if you would like to use any of the other features that they offer.

There is an alternative to viewing your credit score, and that is when you use a credit repair company. Some enjoy having a team of people dedicated to helping them boost their credit score, but others prefer to take matters into their own hands. Know that you can always do this yourself if you do not want to rely on a separate service. When you realize that you do have this option, this is going to make you feel like you are even more in charge of your credit score and what happens to it.

Much like your credit report, you should not feel the need to check your credit score obsessively. This is what will lead you to stress and worry. While your score can change frequently, it is not going to change hourly or daily. Understand that keeping up with your credit score responsibly means that you should have an idea of what it is while keeping in mind that it will fluctuate. Depending on your spending habits, payment upkeep, and factors considered by CRAs, your score can look different all across the board at any given time. In addition, you now know that you can have a few different types of credit scores, like your FICO score or your VantageScore.

- **Never Make a Late Payment**: By continuing to stress on the importance of paying on time, you will learn how to never make a late payment on your credit card or loan. This is one of the biggest ways to make a negative impact on your credit score and it doesn't take long at all. Not only are you going to be hurting your score when you do this, but your creditor might take action that they see fit. Some companies will actually increase your minimum payment until you can prove to them you are going to continue to pay on time.

Naturally, this could put you in a tough spot, especially if you missed your payment because you did not have the funds in the first place. This is why calling your creditor when you know you are going to be late is the smartest decision. When you can inform them ahead of time, this is showing financial responsibility in a new way. You are on top of your finances, so you will be able to see that the funds are going to be short by the time the bill is due.

It isn't a guarantee, but some creditors will allow you to pay later, or break your payments up into smaller installments. They want to work with you because they do not want to suffer a loss, either. When you show that you are willing to communicate with them, they are going to be more likely to cut you a break. Again, there are no guarantees, but it is worth it to try. Many people panic when they realize that they aren't going to be able to make their payment on time.

It can also feel embarrassing because they would rather go without paying than ask a loved one for financial help.

To put this into perspective, if you were to miss your monthly payment and go without paying until your next due date, this can cost you anywhere from 90–110 points knocked off your credit score. This would be a detrimental loss that might have been avoided if you had called your creditor in advance or planned your finances wisely. When you take your credit seriously, you are going to be more likely to take care of it. Understand that it is not just a random number that is assigned to you, but an indication that creditors are going to look at to determine if you are trustworthy enough to borrow money.

When you have money put aside for emergencies , it can really help you out. With each paycheck, try to set aside around 10% of it to put into savings. Tell yourself that you won't use it unless it is absolutely necessary. If a situation comes up that makes it impossible for you to make your payment on time, you will have this money set aside for this exact purpose. What you don't use each month can then be considered savings. It is like you are saving for two purposes, both of which will financially benefit you. Many Americans do not have enough savings to cover situations like these, and it is always better to start saving sooner rather than later. Give yourself the peace of mind to know that you are going to be able to pay your bills, no matter what.

- **Create a Disciplined Routine**: The first step to staying on track of your credit card bills, loan payments, and other bills is being aware of when they are due. Keep track of this on a personal calendar or use an app that can help you. There are plenty of free apps designed to input all your billing information so you will always know what is coming up. They can even send you reminders when the due dates are getting closer and pay your bills through the app. When you are always aware of your bills, you are going to minimize your chances of missing your payments.

If you can set your payments up on auto-pay, this will also be helpful for creating a routine. Since the money is going to come out automatically, all you will need to do is make sure that you have enough money in your account when the payment is due. Auto-pay creates discipline in your routine because it encourages you to save up the money that should be used for paying bills rather than spending it. If you pay all of your bills on your own time, it can be tempting to see that extra money in your account and use it, thinking that you are going to be able to make up for it by the time your bill is due.

Part of keeping your bills down also includes reframing your money-spending habits. When you are tempted to use your credit card to buy something that you don't have the money for, weigh your options. While you will be able to have the instant gratification of making your purchase, think about the cost. Not only are you going to have to pay your creditor back, but you are also going to be charged with interest if you do not pay it off all at once. When you add up all the interest that you are paying on your credit card bills, you will see how much more you are actually paying your creditors than what you truly owe. If you can wait to make your purchase with money that you have in hand, then you will not have to worry about being in debt.

When you create a routine for paying your bills, they are going to feel less like tasks. A task is usually something that takes effort and is difficult. Your goal is to make your bill-paying routine feel just like any other normal part of your week. It doesn't have to be a challenge if you plan well for your due dates. Getting into this kind of routine does take some self-discipline. You might feel like you are giving up some things you want to buy, but it is all going to benefit you in the long run. When you no longer have to worry about ruining your credit score because you cannot pay your bills, you are actually going to come out on top and with more money. The money that you end up saving during this process is going to build up in your account.

If necessary, take your credit cards out of your wallet so that you are not tempted to use them. Staying disciplined can be hard if the cards are still in there. Give them to your spouse or someone you trust to keep them safe for you. When you do not know where they are or how to access them, there is no chance that you are going to overuse them. This is a more drastic measure, but it can prove to be helpful if you feel that you are still struggling with spending too much money on your credit cards.

- **Keep Your Utilization Low**: If you can keep your credit utilization rate under 30%, this is going to reflect well on your credit score. As you know, when you use some credit but not all that you are given, you are going to be showing your creditors that you can use it well. If you notice that your credit utilization rate is becoming too high, you can take this as a sign that your credit score is going to be impacted. Of course, this is possible to repair. You must do your best to stop spending money on this account. The more you spend, the higher your utilization rate is going to be.

Keep in mind that using a different card is not like starting from a 0% utilization rate. This rate is going to keep adding up the more you spend on any card. It considers all of your spending to provide creditors with an overall picture of how much you are using your credit to make purchases. There are different strategies you can use to get your utilization rate down. You can try them all to see which one works best for you.

The first way is by paying off all your credit cards a little at a time. When you can make payments that are slightly over your minimum payments due, this is going to make an improvement on your balances and your utilization rate. Some people like to do this because they feel that they are paying off all of their cards equally, but this can depend on how much of a balance you have on each one. If you pay $50 on a card with a $300 balance versus a card with a $1,500 balance, this does not mean that both of your cards will be paid off at the same time.

Another strategy is by focusing on one card at a time. While maintaining your other minimum payments, pick one card that you have with a balance that you'd like to pay off. This can be because the balance is high or because the interest rate is adding too much money to your payments. Once you have your focus set, pay extra on this card each month to get the balance down. When you do this, you will also be keeping your utilization rate down. No matter how you'd like to distribute your funds, you can choose the best option for your lifestyle.

If you have any maxed-out credit cards, this can hurt your credit score by around 10–45 points. Not to mention, you are always going to feel stressed out knowing that you have a card that has reached its limit. Of course, if you do have any maxed-out cards, you should prioritize those when you are thinking about how you are going to repay your debt. Try not to let this get you too worried or stressed because there is only one thing that you can do now — pay off your cards. Since it isn't possible for you to spend any more money on them, you can put all of your focus on paying them off successfully.

- **Pay More Than the Minimum**: The importance of this step was discussed earlier, and it is one of the best things that you can do for your credit score — pay more than the minimum amount due if you are able. Not only are you keeping your utilization rates low when you do this, but you are also lowering the amount of interest that is placed onto your monthly payments. Because interest rates work on a percentage basis, the higher your balance, the more interest you are going to be charged. When you can pay more than your minimum due, even if you are not paying your card off, you are still benefiting from that lower interest rate.

Even if you can only manage to pay an additional $10, that is a starting point. Make a goal to pay an extra $10 on all of your credit card bills this month. You might have to give up some small things, but nothing that should impact your life in a major way. Sometimes, making coffee at home a few days a week instead of purchasing it is all it takes to obtain that extra money that you can put toward your credit cards. By getting into these better spending habits, you are also going to be less likely to create another high balance on your card.

If you can handle it, start paying an additional $20 on each credit card bill in the months to follow. This process can be gradual, giving you enough time to adjust to your new lifestyle. You might also have to continue giving up small things you don't need to meet this goal. A few nights of staying in for dinner instead of eating out can give you the extra money that you need. It can also help to start bringing your lunch from home because ordering take out at work is one big way that people tend to waste money. The following are some other ideas that you can use to make sure you are saving money where you can:

- Have your friends over at your house instead of going out with them. This gives you the chance to spend time together with them while saving the money that you would've spent at a bar or a restaurant.

- Watch a movie at home and make your spouse dinner instead of going out to do the same. You can have meaningful date nights at home without sacrificing any of the things that you like to do together.

- Get the kids to put together a list of their favorite meals. Place these options in a jar and let them take turns picking one out each day. This will make eating at home a little more exciting and they will be eating the food that they love.

- Save your coins in a jar each time you make a purchase and get change back. After a few months, you can cash in these coins and put the money toward your credit card payments.

- Take a closer look at where your spending money is going. If you have many subscriptions, now is the time to rethink them and consider if they are actually bringing any value into your life. If you are no longer enjoying them, then you can save money by canceling them and put the money toward your cards.

- **Limit New Loan Inquiries**: It can be tempting to know what loans you qualify for, especially when you notice that your credit score is improving. You need to be careful with how many loans you apply for because this can become a big reason for why your credit score goes back down again. Thinking back on the different types of inquiries, remember that loan applications usually run hard inquiries. This will cause your score to drop, especially if you apply for them too frequently.

The same can be said about refinancing. It does not make sense to go for a refinance every other month because there is likely very little that your creditor will be able to offer you. When you refinance, your creditor has to see that you have a history of making on time payments and a steady credit score for them to consider lowering your balance and payments. It would be a better idea to see what your options are every other year or so. At this rate, your credit score would not suffer much.

Remember that loan shopping is not a great thing to do. It is important that you are well-informed, but actually applying for a loan is a big step that you must be ready for. Before you apply, ask yourself if you truly need the loan and consider how it would help you. Next, you need to remember that the loan is going to come with terms. How long do you have to pay this off and how much interest are you going to have to pay? Make sure you consider the fact that any promotional offers that provide you with 0% interest are going to end, eventually. The interest rate that you are left with is often going to be high.

- **Use Multiple Credit Types**: Do your best to create some variety within your credit portfolio. Many people obtain a lot of credit cards when they want to boost their score but consider how an auto loan or a home loan will fare. You do not need to stack up on only one type of credit to raise your score and doing so only for this purpose will likely only put you deeper into debt. The types of credit that you use should be beneficial to you, helping some aspect of your life. It is never a good idea to take a credit card offer just because you are given one.

Once you get started on your credit journey, you are going to be given many offers to open more accounts. You might notice that you start getting more of these in the mail the higher that your balances get. This can become dangerous when you feel that the offers are starting to look beneficial. Know that adding more to your debt when you are already drowning in it is never a good idea, even if the interest rate is low or non-existent.

When stores try to get you to sign up for their credit cards, they make the experience feel a lot more casual. Because you typically get approved on the spot, it can be a great feeling to know that you are able to get this line of credit so easily. The store will also usually offer you a discount on your purchase if you sign up for their card at that moment. The idea of being able to get 20% off might be tempting but know that this is still a credit card that is going to impact your credit score and leave you with a balance to pay off. Even if you didn't have to wait days for approval, it still works the same way and can easily get you into debt.

It is important that you do not just close your accounts after you pay them off, as mentioned. When you do not owe money on your account, yet you paid some money off previously, this will show lenders you have the self-discipline to have the credit lines available to you, but that you do not necessarily *need to* use them. If your credit card has been paid off and it is just sitting in your wallet, this is not going to cause your credit score to go down. Use it occasionally and pay it off right away if you do not want to accumulate debt, but do not get rid of it.

Once you get to a place where you are able to fund purchases without having to use credit, you can still opt to use credit to build your score up. For example, you can make a purchase of a new television on credit and then pay it off with the money that you have saved up as soon as you receive your bill. This is going to boost your score and it will still keep your credit card debt-free once you pay off the balance. Buying the television this way is the same as just paying for it with the money that you have saved, but you will also be boosting your credit score in the process. Small steps like this will allow you to see a major improvement in your score.

Chapter 6: Don't Get Scared, Start That Credit Score Repair

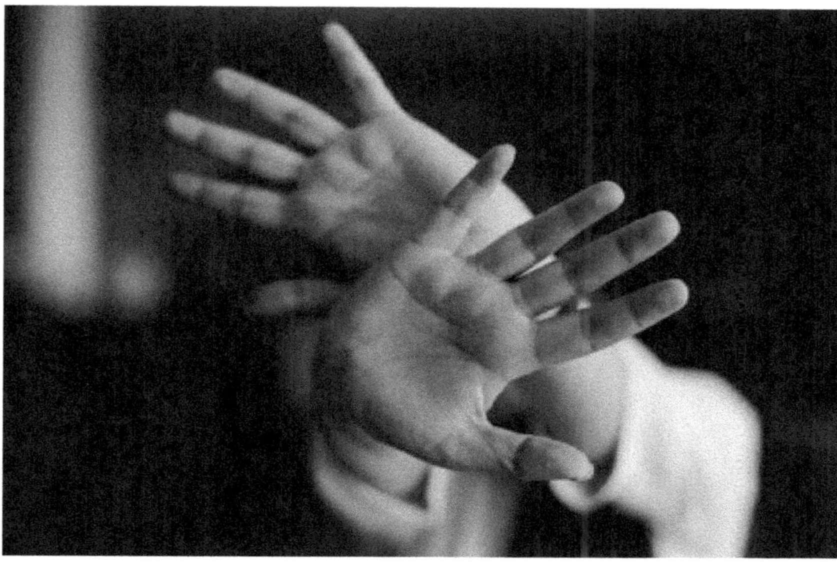

Fear

Credit repair is necessary when you have damaged your score to the point where it is in a lower range than it used to be. During the process of credit repair, you will ideally be removing negative items from your credit report. Because this can happen easily, many people find themselves in this position, unsure of what to do next. You might begin to panic, wondering if you are ever going to be able to display a credit score that you are proud of again. With enough hard work, you will. Your credit score can be repaired, and you will be able to avoid getting into this same situation again in the future. This chapter is going to look at everything you need to know about credit repair and how to make it work for you.

Despite common misconceptions, you do not need to pay a service to repair your score for you. This can actually be done yourself with the steps that are going to be provided. When you have these tools and this knowledge, you won't need to put your credit score in the hands of other people. Instead, you will be able to take pride in knowing that you were able to get your score back into a range that you can feel proud of. By taking these steps, you will be able to maximize your score and put you in an overall better financial standing. All the stress and worry that surrounds having a bad score will no longer be able to hold you back.

Does Credit Repair Work?

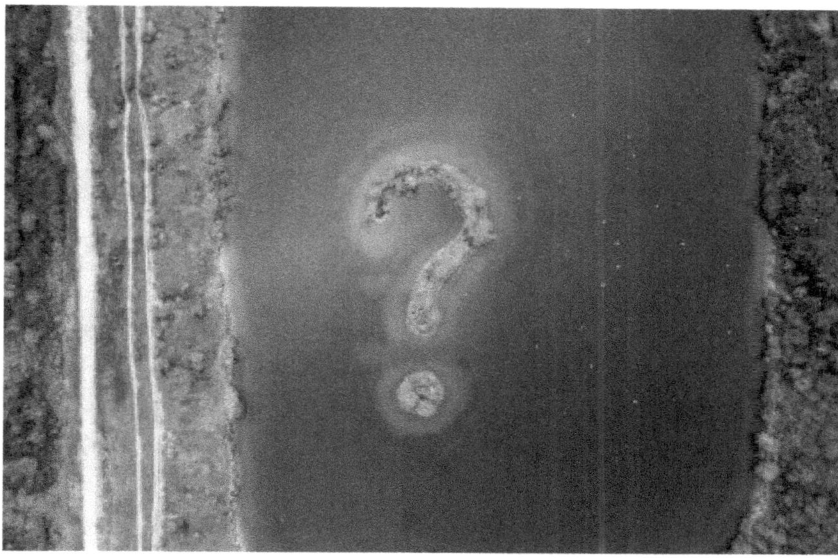

Question Mark

Credit repair is not a magic fix that is going to give you a perfect credit score instantly. It is a process that is going to take time and get better depending on how much experience you have. You are likely going to learn a lot along the way, and this is how you are going to gain valuable experience. Part of credit repair involves removing certain negative items from your credit report. Know that credit repair will not work for every type of item, though. As long as it can be disputed, this usually indicates that credit repair is going to work for your account. While looking at your credit report, you will be repairing it by going down the list of items and disputing the ones you feel are inaccurate or unfair.

When your report is no longer filled with false or inaccurate information, this will allow you to improve your credit score because the CRAs will only be using the information that correctly reflects your credit history. Sometimes, false data can appear on your credit report when your information has been involved in a data breach. Unfortunately, this can happen at any time. Internet security is never going to be able to protect you fully, but the good thing is that you should be able to dispute these items. This is one reason why regularly reading your credit report will benefit you. If you notice anything that you are not sure of, you can always ask.

Credit repair is not something that you can use to dispute ordinary charges or items on your account that you were responsible for. This would be illegal and considered fraudulent. On top of this, if you were to dispute something ordinary, it is almost a guarantee that it would be rejected. A credit bureau is not going to spend the time looking into something that can be easily explained. The following items are the ones that are most likely to be successfully disputed:

- **Erroneous Items**: This type of item is generally easy to dispute because it is just flat-out wrong. Some examples of an erroneous item include a misspelling or a misreported amount. Usually, erroneous items are more like nuances that can cause confusion on your credit report. They are easy to fix and will likely be taken care of in a timely manner. Another example of an erroneous item that can cause a lot more damage to your credit score would be a misplaced decimal point. If you owe $60.00 and the item reads $600.00, this is going to make a big difference in your credit utilization and your debt owed. When you see a mistake like this, dispute it right away.

- **Outdated Items**: This is another item that is likely going to be easy for you to dispute. As it sounds, an outdated item no longer applies to you because it happened so long ago. While most items only appear on your credit report for a certain amount of time before they are removed, those months or years can still make a difference on your credit score. The sooner you are able to get rid of anything that is outdated, the sooner you are going to see this reflected in your score. If you notice a hard inquiry or a late payment appearing on your report, make sure you verify that it should still be there. It can be outdated if the hard inquiry is still there after two years and if the late payment is still impacting your score after seven years. Every item should have a maximum age and it doesn't hurt to research this.

- **Fraudulent Items**: These items usually appear on your credit report after you have been a victim of identity theft. This is one of the worst things that can happen to you. Not only can there be fraudulent transactions on your credit report, but there also might be fraudulent accounts. If you never recall opening the account, then do not assume that you did this and simply forgot about it. There is a chance that you have been a victim of identity theft temporarily. Someone else might have used your information to open an account and then close it before you could bring it to the creditor's attention. The account can look legitimate and even be through a creditor you know of, but its origins will tell you more. When you dispute something like this, the account will be investigated to give you an idea of how it was opened in the first place.

- **Unsubstantiated Items**: This kind of item would be something that the information providers cannot substantiate. For example, if there is a debt that they are insisting belongs to you, yet you know that it does not, they won't be able to have any further information to back this up. This is an unsubstantiated item, and it can definitely be disputed. As long as they are not able to provide any additional information that shows you are responsible for the debt or negative mark, the credit bureaus will usually be able to remove them from your credit report.

Now that you are able to familiarize yourself with the different types of actions you can take to help repair your credit, you will see that this is a niche practice. You need to know what to look for and how to contact the people who are in charge. Most places that allow you to view your credit report make it super easy to file a dispute. There will typically be a number that you can call or a link that you can click that will allow you to make a dispute electronically. Make sure you keep track of the disputes you make because this can help you catch them sooner in the future.

Credit repair is a step that goes beyond spending your credit responsibly and paying your bills on time. It allows you to become more proactive on your credit journey and shows you that small mistakes can cause a lot of damage to your credit score. As long as you are making your disputes carefully, you can make credit repair a beneficial part of your maintenance routine. Keep in mind that you should check all three credit reports before you assume that your reports are all clear. Some credit reports are not going to report the same information; therefore, you might only find errors on one instead of all three.

You aren't going to be able to predict which credit report will be viewed when a creditor needs to look at one, so it is important that you do your best to keep track of them all. By taking this additional preventative measure, you can feel confident that your credit reports are all in good standing and displaying the correct information. Going from only knowing what you are told to realizing that you can dispute information that does not appear to be correct is a very empowering feeling. This is your chance to take back all the stress and worry that your credit report has caused in your life.

What to Expect

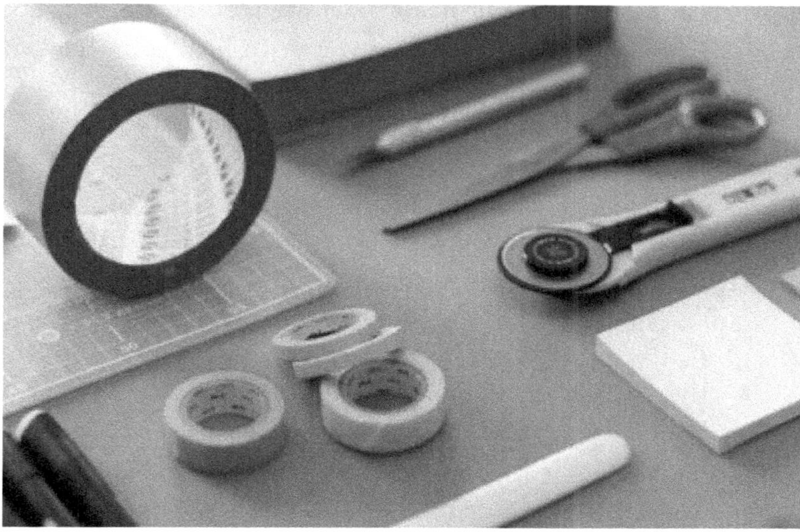

Tools

You should know that it is within your legal right to dispute inaccurate items on your credit report. The Fair Credit Reporting Act (FCRA) backs this for all consumers. The FCRA is a federal law that was put into place that helps to ensure that your information is accurate, fair, and private. This law also regulates how the CRAs collect your information. It helps to protect you from getting your private information exposed to dangerous third-party companies. The CRAs are only supposed to collect it to compile your credit reports, not to sell it for a profit. You can rest assured that you have the FCRA on your side when you are working on the credit repair process.

Established in 1970, the FCRA became a liaison to consumers to educate them better on what could be done regarding the changing or disputing of information on their credit reports. Because information is constantly being gathered, other companies outside of the three main

CRAs might collect and use your information. In some cases, this is harmless and justified. An example of this would be your bank accessing your information because you have applied for a loan. However, in other cases, this is how identity theft begins. It is up to the FCRA to support you and help you get a handle on how your information is being distributed.

The following are some other ways that the FCRA aims to help you:

- The FCRA allows you to be informed when information in your credit file was used against you if you are denied an application.

- The FCRA gives you the right to request a "file disclosure," of all the information a consumer reporting agency has about you. You can get one free file disclosure annually.

- The FCRA gives you the chance to opt-out of any pre-screened credit offers that you receive.

- The FCRA can put a security freeze on your credit report if necessary. This means that potential lenders will not be able to view your credit report until you give the FCRA permission to lift the freeze. You also have the option of creating a personalized pin that you can give to the lender that you'd like to give permission to view your reports.

In the past, it was required that you put your disputes in writing and mail them in. This time-consuming process has since been updated in the age of technology. Now, almost every dispute can be made online from home. All you need to do is go to the given credit bureau's website. Finding the error and submitting the dispute is only the first half of the credit repair process. After you do this, you need to keep in mind that you might have to wait awhile before you hear anything back from them. For common disputes, you can expect them to be handled fairly quickly. Depending on the complexity of your situation, the disputes can take more time.

You need to file a separate dispute for each item that you would like to change. This means that a misspelling in your name and an outdated debt appearing on your report would have to be made in two separate disputes. If you find that this information is incorrect on all three of your credit reports, you will have to file them accordingly per report. This is why the process of credit repair can be time-consuming, but it will be worth it when you have the confidence that all your reported information is correct.

Make sure you gather as many details as possible when you file your disputes. You need to include as many supporting documents as you can because this is going to help provide a clear picture of why you are filling the dispute. Note that dates and exact dollar amounts are also going to be helpful. When you do send in evidentiary documents, make sure you send copies. You should always keep the originals for your own file. Having a paper trail is especially important because you will not have to spend as much time explaining why you are filing the dispute. Moreover, it is more reputable when you have an official document that is stating why you need to make a change and why certain information might be incorrect.

After you submit your dispute, you will be given a confirmation. Keep this in your file. It is also important to keep any correspondence that you might have along the way. This is going to allow you to stay organized and keep track of each one of your disputes. In case any problems arise, you will also have written proof of the dispute you have submitted and anything that you were told. After you submit a dispute to a bureau, they have 30 days to investigate it. They will not always take this long depending on the complexity of the dispute, but they can take the full 30 days, if necessary. One requirement is that the agency must forward your dispute and the information that you have provided to the given party in question.

After the information is investigated, the results must be reported back to the credit bureau. If it is found that the information was indeed incorrect, it is required that all three credit bureaus be notified, and they are requested to be removed. Once the investigation has concluded, the credit bureau needs to inform you of the results in an official letter. They are also supposed to provide you with a copy of the items that have been changed or corrected. If anyone has received your credit report in the last six months, you can request to have the credit bureau send them a notice that states there have been corrections or changes made.

Statistics

As mentioned, the credit repair process is not something that is supposed to be a quick fix for your credit score. It can help tremendously, but you have to be willing to go through the process. According to statistics, it takes around nine months to 2 ½ years for someone to bounce back after their credit score has gone down. This just shows how easy it can be to damage your score and how much work it takes to get it back to what it was. It also shows that the process is not going to happen in vain.

Even with the process of credit repair as a valid option, experts still advise that the number one way to raise your credit score is by making timely payments. If you can help it, do your best to make sure that you never miss a payment and you could be saving yourself the loss of 100 points from your credit score. This is still proven to be the easiest and fast method of taking care of your credit score.

In 2019, FICO stated that the consumers who had scores between 720 and 850 were seen as ideal. They were the ones who qualified for lower interest rates and better credit card offers. These statistics are always changing, but you can use this as a guideline for the score you'd like to aim for.

When it comes to having a perfect credit score, only a small percentage of the country has one. It is said that less than 1% of the entire population can say that they have a perfect credit score. While it can be nice to set high goals, know that having a perfect score isn't essential or necessary. As it has been reported in the last year, around 20% of the population has a credit score of 700+. This shows that the average is not going to be near perfect, but closer to fair.

Steps to Take

Now that you have an idea of how to get started with your credit repair journey, you can use the following steps as a guideline to help you make the process more streamlined. You can follow these steps to make any type of dispute that you need to make. While you cannot guarantee the results, you will at least have the peace of mind that you have done everything on your end that is required of you. These are the most common methods taken by consumers that tend to bring forth positive results.

1. Reading is your very first step. You need to read your credit reports regularly. Now that you know how many there are and where you can obtain them, it is up to you to pay close attention to them. Even if you haven't had any new activity on your credit report in the last few months, there are still chances of inconsistencies appearing. When you get used to reading them frequently, you are going to be able to immediately spot these inconsistencies and get them all to match up. Make sure to take note of any negative items on your reports and how long they have been there because none of them should stay on your reports forever.

Remember that you have the right to dispute information on all three of your reports and that, sometimes, certain information will not appear on all of them. This is why it is essential that you read over each one individually, paying attention to any small errors that might pop up. Even an error like a misspelling is worth making a dispute over because this might complicate things for you in the future when you fill out applications or apply for more credit.

1. To write out your dispute, you can follow this template:

- Include your name, address, and contact information.

- Make sure you also include the date.

- Address the dispute to the correct bureau, using their contact information if you plan to mail them the correspondence.

- Tell them that you are writing to dispute the information in your file.

- Attach a copy of the report you have received and mark it with the error that you found. Indicate that you have circled the error that you wish to address in the attached report.

- Identify the item by the name of the creditor, the amount given, and the information provided. Be very detailed about this part.

- Explain *why* the information is incorrect and needs to be changed. Provide your corrections, if necessary, provide your corrections.

- Include any supporting documents that you have to clarify your issue.

- At the end of the email, clarify what you have enclosed or attached.

1. Once you submit all the information that you have, you must give the CRA up to 30 days to perform their investigation. While they might be able to work through it more quickly

depending on the complexity of the issue, you should still expect it to take around one month. For simple errors like misspellings and such, you can probably count on these being corrected a lot sooner than a debt that has been assigned to you that you are actually not responsible for.

Because you are now familiar with some of the most common types of disputes that are made, you should have a general idea of the timeline that you can expect. Remember that there are four different types: erroneous, outdated, fraudulent, and unsubstantial. If you notice more than one error on a report, you will have to submit the disputes separately. This can allow you to get your issues taken care of sooner. If you have one misspelling on your report and one outdated debt, the former will be fixed first since it will be on its own dispute and it will prevent you from having to wait a long time to get them both handled.

1. You have help on your side that comes from the Consumer Financial Protection Bureau (CFPB). If you find that the CRA is not being cooperative for whatever reason, you can contact the CFPB to help you. Remember, it is your legal right to be able to dispute errors on your credit reports if you find them. There are many reasons as to why the CRA might be difficult to work with, but this does not mean that you should just give up on finding the answers that you are entitled to or getting the corrections made.

If you believe that your dispute isn't being handled correctly, or if it is taking well over the 30 days that it should, you can contact the CFPB to determine what your next step should be. They will be able to listen to your case and provide you individualized answers that you can use to take action. Many people feel they are lost and confused in the process of making disputes, which is why they might not have tried to do so in the past. Know that you do not have to settle for unfinished disputes or inaccurate answers.

1. When it comes to credit repair, anyone should be able to do this on his or her own. Now that you are familiar with what the process entails and how to get in touch with the right people, you should be able to comb through your reports and decide for yourself when and if you need to make any disputes. It isn't hard to do, as long as you are able to pay attention to the finer details and compare your reports regularly.

If the task becomes more than you can handle, there are agencies that can help you with your credit repair journey. These agencies will make the correspondence for you, but they are going to charge you a fee for doing so. When using one, you will still have to gather as much information as you can about what you'd like to dispute and why. If you'd rather have them keep up with your disputes and handle any correspondences, then you might feel more comfortable paying the fee and allowing them to process your information for you.

1. If you think about it, paying a fee to an agency that will work on this process for you is kind of like being robbed of money that you do not need to spend. While the services can sound convenient at first, consider that you are still going to have to take the time to read your reports and gather all the information that might be incorrect or inaccurate.

Take time to look over your reports and you will not feel as stressed out by the process. Without having to spend any money, you can obtain the reports and read them over. Because you already know this information best, you will not have to explain things more than once when you handle the credit repair process on your own. If you do run into any issues that you cannot get through by yourself, you can always use the services the CFPB provides.

1. If you have many disputes to make or if they are complex in nature, then it might be worthwhile to seek out the help of a credit repair agency that you can pay. Most people find that they need the extra help when they are going to be applying for a mortgage or an auto loan because these fall into a category that is more major than something like a new credit card. If you have no plans in the near future to apply for a big loan, then it isn't worth it to spend money on hiring a credit repair agency. In addition, if you have big negative marks on your credit report that cannot be disputed (like a bankruptcy), you already know that this is going to stay on the report for a certain amount of time. There would be no need to hire an agency to clear anything like this up unless the item becomes outdated.

No matter how many times you have gone through a credit repair process in the past, it is always a good idea to revisit this if it has been a couple of months. A lot can change in that time and around 20% of people that check their credit reports found mistakes that they would not have otherwise noticed. This information was lowering their score and they could have fixed it a lot sooner had they been more willing to look into the details of their credit report. Being observant does not come with a cost, so it is worthwhile to turn this into a habit that you can rely on.

Chapter 7: Bringing It All Together

Circle

Now that you have taken a comprehensive look at what it takes to boost your credit score, you should feel like you have a better idea of how you can apply some of these strategies to your life. It can be hard to know where to begin, but with the resources that you already have available to you, it does not have to be a stressful or confusing process. In this chapter, all the important information that you have learned will be compiled in one place for you to reference. Whenever you need to refresh your memory on what to do next, you can always look at this chapter for an easy way to keep your credit score maintenance under control.

You don't have to be an expert to make a noticeable difference in your credit score. As you have seen, most of the steps that must be taken involve patience and observation. By making it a point to focus on the goal of improving your score, you should be able to work with the details you have and create focused habits that will get you to exactly where you want to be. Remember, your credit score matters. It can give you access to credit lines and loans that will make your life easier and more enjoyable. Your credit score paints a picture of your financial history that lenders are going to continue to view. You should be proud of how you are being represented, especially when you are working hard to maintain your credit score.

A Review

Studying

- Know the differences between your credit history, credit reports, and credit scores. Because you can obtain them all from a few different sources, it should be noted that the information isn't always going to be identical. When you can view all of them regularly, this is going to give you the insight that you will need to improve your credit score and make disputes when necessary. By having free access to all these things annually, you should not have to pay any fees or spend any additional time searching for ways to obtain them. With your credit score, viewing it has become even easier now that many banks and credit card companies allow you to view it anytime you want.

Now that you are aware of the different credit reports and the different credit scores that represent you, it does not have to be an end-all feeling when you find that there is something that could use improvement on one. As you view these things, you will probably find that there are many things that could use improvement, but that is how you are going to find the motivation to raise your credit score. Don't let it take control of your life any longer. You have the ability to change it because you know the steps to take now. Your credit does not have to be a dark cloud that lingers over your head.

- Your credit score is not only calculated by a single factor. The first way to secure a high credit score is by making your payments on time. Your payment history is the most definitive factor because it makes up the highest percentage of your score. Next, you need to keep in mind your credit utilization rate. Any amount that is 30% or lower, this is going to boost your credit score. It will show that you can use your credit within a responsible range. Lenders want to know that you are using it, so they would prefer you to have some reported utilization rather than a 0% rate.

The length of your credit history is also going to be taken into consideration. If you have only just opened a credit card account this year, you aren't going to have much experience with credit yet. The CRAs are going to take this into account while they are calculating your score. The only way to improve the length of your credit history is by keeping accounts open for a long time. This is why it is better to keep your accounts open, even if they are paid off or if you are not using them. This is going to count toward improving your credit score.

Your recent activity is going to highlight how many times inquiries have been run on your account. If you have many hard inquiries not only will this lower your score by a few points each time, but it will also show that you are frequently applying for credit. Try to only apply for a loan or a credit card when you are certain that you need it and that you have a high chance of being approved. The final aspect of your credit score revolves around your credit mix. This shows how many types of credit you have, from credit cards to auto loans. A variety can be a good thing.

- Having a good credit score means that you will be given many benefits that can help make your life easier. One of the first is a lower interest rate. Your interest rate matters so much because it is going to add up over time the longer you keep a balance. Most cards offer introductory rates that can be as low as 0%, but this usually does not last for too long. Once that period is up, you might be facing up to 20% in interest, which means that 20% is going to be added to your balance each month that it is not paid off. By the time that you eventually pay it off, this is going to add quite a bit of extra money to the amount that you originally owed.

Another benefit is qualifying for faster loan approval. When you have a good score, this is going to show lenders that they can trust you and that you have experience. They are going to be more likely to approve someone in a timely manner with a good credit score than someone with a low credit score. In addition to this, you are also going to be offered higher credit limits when you have a better score. You never know when you might need to use credit, so having an abundance of it can really help you. When you don't have a good credit score, you might struggle to get enough credit to fund your purchases.

Finally, a good credit score can also mean lower bills. Many companies from your cell phone provider to your utility bill run your credit to see that you are going to be able to pay your bills on time. The higher your score, the more discounts you will be given. Even your insurance company might discount your premium if they see that you have an admirable credit score. Without the credit score to back you up, many companies will not feel comfortable allowing you to open accounts with them. They might require that you create an account with someone who has a better score for them to feel that you are not going to be a liability.

- Make sure you are aware of all the myths that surround your credit score. There are a few of them that are still currently circulating that you might have heard. Not only are they untrue, but they might lead you in the wrong direction as you attempt to work on boosting your credit score. The sooner you are able to debunk these myths, the sooner you will be able to fix your credit score. Remember the following:

1. Not all debt is equal. Owing $100,000 on a home mortgage is not the same as owing $100,000 in credit card bills. Remember that there are two types of credit: revolving and installment. With the former, you are given a credit limit, but you are choosing how much to spend on that limit. This is how credit cards typically work and this is why it can be easy to get into credit card debt if you do not practice self-discipline.

Your installment credit accounts will make up your home loans and auto loans. This is an agreed-upon amount that is put into place for the sole purpose of paying off one item, such as a home or a vehicle. Once you pay the amount off in full, the debt goes away, and you cannot spend any additional money on that loan. This is why you cannot consider all debts to be equal.

1. If you pay off your debt instantly, this does not mean that you are going to maximize your credit score. If you have the option, show that you can make regular monthly payments. This is going to benefit you in a few ways. For one, it is going to be the most significant way to boost your credit score. This is what your credit score revolves around, so it will benefit you greatly. When you take the time to make monthly payments, you are also going to be keeping your utilization rate at a steady level and showing lenders that you use your credit cards responsibly.

Plus, when you take some time to pay your bills, your account is active and counting toward the length of your account history. If you would like to pay more than the minimum amount due, that is great, but know that paying off your debt in a lump sum isn't always going to benefit you how you think it will. If necessary, keep that money saved for the purpose of paying off your debt and continue to make your regular monthly payments.

1. Your job, marital status, and amount of money saved will not have any impact on your credit score. CRAs do not look into your personal information in this way. No matter if you are currently employed by a large company or working for yourself, this won't make a difference in how high your credit

score is. While you do have the ability to receive certain discounts if you are married, this will not directly impact your score. Your finances are not a direct reflection of your credit score because they can change in an instant. CRAs will not need to know how much money you have in the bank.

Because nothing personal is involved in the matter, this will remind you to set your focus on getting your payments to your lender on time and keeping your utilization rate low. When you do this, you will notice more of an impact on your credit score than anything else that you try. This is not difficult to accomplish when you create a routine for yourself that forces you to use your credit responsibly.

1. When you have no debt, this is not equivalent to having the perfect credit score. To boost your credit score, you do need to use credit. Those who first start out without ever having credit before are typically under the misconception that they start with a maximum score. This isn't true — you start with a low score and have the opportunity to build it up. This is why most people without any credit have a hard time renting a property, financing homes, and finding credit card companies who are willing to approve them.

The same can be said for when you pay off your debt — just because you are currently debt-free does not mean that your score will automatically be maximized. You still need to work on building it, which means using your credit and paying it back in a responsible manner. Keep your accounts open and keep using them periodically. This is going to be the best way to boost your credit score quickly.

1. It does not take a long time to ruin your credit score. While it

does take a long time for your score to build up, you can ruin it as easy as making two late payments. When this happens, you are at risk of hurting your score by up to 100 points. It takes longer to build it back up because you need to prove to your lender that you can be responsible for your spending habits and this takes time. They want to see that you have a pattern of borrowing money and paying it back in a consistent and timely fashion.

When people believe that it takes a long time to ruin their credit score, they also forget that spending copious amounts of money on credit can be a blow to their score. When you rack up a lot of debt in a fairly short amount of time, this is likely going to take you a while to pay off. Remember, your credit utilization rate goes both ways. Once you surpass the 30% mark, this is going to begin hurting your credit score. You need to keep it balanced to show your lenders you are using just the right amount.

1. Loan shopping, or frequently applying for loans, is not going to boost your credit score. In fact, this is going to hurt it. The more you apply for loans, the more you will be given hard inquiries on your account. As you know, this lowers your credit score a little each time. Applying for a loan is a big decision that you should take your time to research. Most have pre-approval requirements to give you an idea if the loan is going to be the right fit for you.

Only apply for the loan if you really need it. If you plan on paying off credit card debt with a personal loan, this is like going into debt in an attempt to pay off debt — it will usually not result in the outcome you are hoping for. A loan should be taken out before you make a big purchase, such as putting yourself through school or buying a car. Keep this in mind before you send out all of your applications.

1. Your credit score does not serve as an indication of how good of a person you are. The traits that you possess and the skills that you have should not be compared to the three-digit number of your credit score. The kindest people can have bad credit, just as the most terrible people can have great credit. The factors do not discriminate. Your lenders just want to know that you can be responsible with your usage and pay your bills on time. They do not look into what you do in your personal life or how you spend your free time.

Taking away the stigma of thinking you are a bad person because you have a low credit score is going to alleviate you of your stress. There can be a lot of pressure to boost your score because it can impact many areas of your life. While this is true, this does not mean that you aren't a great person because your score isn't quite where you'd like it to be. This takes time and hard work. If you are willing to put in the effort, then you are going to be able to see the results in a given time.

- Credit repair is a process you can undergo that has the potential to boost your credit score. It involves obtaining your credit reports and reviewing them, paying close attention to all the details. If you notice a mistake or an inaccuracy, this can be hurting your credit score without you even realizing it. You have the right to dispute items that you believe are either erroneous, outdated, fraudulent, or unsubstantiated. To do this, you would make a dispute with the given CRA that gave you the report. Note that not all of your credit reports are going to reflect the same information, which is why it is important to read through all of them for mistakes.

The CRA then has 30 days to complete an investigation and will look into your dispute but know that they can take less time if the issue is minor. If you ever feel that you are being treated unfairly the Fair Credit Reporting Act is on your side. The FCRA is going to be able to help you if you run into any issues during any of the disputes you make. There are agencies that you can hire to repair your credit for you, but this is usually a waste of money because you can do the same thing by yourself at no charge. You have access to all three of your credit reports annually for free, so all you need to do is read and compare them.

Credit Score Statistics

Percentage

When you are aware of the statistics that surround having a good credit score, you will feel more informed about what it takes to improve your own. There are certain generations that have higher credit scores because they were taught to handle their credit differently. In today's age, there is more information available than ever but there is also a lot of misinformation that is being spread through and resources found on the internet. According to a study by VantageScore, the Silent Generation typically has the highest credit scores among the other generations. Their scores are usually in the 730 range. These individuals were born in the mid-1920s–1940s.

Coming in next is the Baby Boomer generation. Born between 1946–1964, this generation typically holds credit scores of around 700. Still working in chronological order, Generation X (1965–1979) comes in with scores around 655. Finally, Millennials and Generation

Z come in with the lowest credit scores. They range from around 630–634. As you can see, there is quite a divide between the younger and older generations. When you become more informed about how credit works and what you can do to improve your score, you can work on bridging this gap.

Logistically, there are also certain areas where people seem to have higher credit scores and certain areas where people have lower credit scores. According to another survey, states such as Minnesota, Wisconsin, and South Dakota seem to have scores that are in the 700+ range. In states like Mississippi, Georgia, and Texas, the scores are in the 620 range. There are many reasons why this occurs, one of which being the specific socioeconomic conditions in each given area. Where the cost of living is high and the minimum wage is low, it makes sense that people would likely have to rely on credit more, therefore, accumulating a lot of debt. Of course, this isn't true for every person in each given state. Situations can vary from one household to the next.

A study was done on information from 2005 to 2019. It appears that there has been a generally steady increase in good credit scores since the study began. Many would argue that this is happening because people are becoming well-informed about their credit and how to manage it. The average FICO score in October of 2005, according to the study, was 688. In April of 2019, that average had risen to 706. These averages have fluctuated during the last two decades, but it is apparent that there was a spike in good credit scores that occurred between 2017 and 2018 that has been steadily increasing since.

Tips That Will Always Boost Your Score

Rocket

- Make sure that you always review your credit reports. They are easily accessible and free to view, so remind yourself to check on them at least annually. It is a good idea to review your reports before you make a big purchase. The more you stay on top of this information, the more you will be able to spot any mistakes that you would potentially need to dispute. This ensures that you always know what is going on with your credit and what might be impacting your credit score.

- Paying on time should be your number one priority. If you are going to set a focus on one credit score boosting behavior, make sure that all of your payments are made on time. This is going to keep your score steadily rising, and it is going to show your lenders one of the biggest signs of financial responsibility. There are no tricks or gimmicks to paying on time — you just have to remember when your bills are due. If it is easier for you, set your payments up on auto-pay so that you do not forget.

- Create a routine that surrounds your credit usage. If you tell yourself that you are not going to spend as much money on your credit cards, then you need to stick with your plan. Take your cards out of your wallet, if necessary. You can also arrange for your spouse to keep them safe for you if you cannot avoid the temptation of using your cards. Obtaining a credit score that you are proud of takes a lot of self-discipline, but you will get there if you put in the effort. Also, make sure you are not unnecessarily applying for more credit cards or loans. Credit should be used as a backup plan, not as a way to fund your lifestyle. You are going to save yourself from the hassle of debt when you can think of it this way.

- Lower your credit utilization ratio. This can be done in one of two ways, the first being making regular payments on your debts. As you pay off your debts, your credit utilization is going to go down automatically. This has always been the easiest and safest way to lower your ratio. If you want to get it down a little faster, aim to make payments that are slightly higher than your minimum payment due. This is also going to help you with your interest rate since that is based on a percentage of your total balance owed. The second way you can do this is by opening another credit account. This is risky, especially if you do not have a lot of self-control when it comes to spending your credit. However, if you can safely manage to open another credit account, this will improve your utilization ratio because you will have more available credit to use.

- If you are going to have a lot of credit, make sure that you try to add some variety into your portfolio. Having a credit card and a car loan, for example, shows diversity. If you only have five credit cards, this isn't going to do as much for your score as having a few credit cards, student loans, and a car loan. While this isn't always possible, remember that it will help your credit score. Carefully consider your options when you are thinking about opening any type of new credit account.

- Check your credit score for informational purposes. One of the easiest ways to get carried away with boosting your credit score is adding unnecessary stress to your life. When you obsessively check this number, it is always going to stress you out because you are not going to be able to see your progress. You should at least give yourself a few weeks in between each observation that you make, even if your bank or your credit card companies give you access to it every single day. Do not upset yourself by constantly viewing it and wishing that you could do more. Remember, credit card boosting takes time and having a keen eye for detail is what it takes to improve it. Use your score as a tool rather than a definition of who you are as a person.

Conclusion

You should now have all the tools and resources that you need to embark on your credit journey. As you navigate which accounts are useful to you and which offer the best interest rates, you are going to be equipped with the knowledge that you need to make the best financial decisions for your current lifestyle. Remember, just because someone you know has a certain credit score and certain credit accounts doesn't mean that the same methods are going to work for you. Because you are a unique individual with different spending habits and needs, you will need to tailor your credit journey toward your life.

Do not feel bad if your credit score is currently low because it is possible for you to make a significant improvement on it, no matter how bad your debt has gotten. You always have options and now you know how to implement these options successfully. Use the tips and tricks to keep you ahead of your debt and work on your self-discipline so you do not find yourself in even more debt. The average American is consumed not only by debt but thoughts of how they are going to repay this debt. If you are one of these individuals, know that it will get better.

Your credit score is an important aspect of your life, but it does not define your worth. Use the benefits of having a good credit score to keep you motivated and on track. When you think about all the options that will be available to you when you boost your score by even a little, this should keep you striving to raise that number. Acknowledge your achievements because even the smallest ones are going to make a difference in the long run. Each timely payment that you make will lower your balance, lower your interest, and keep your lenders happy.

As stated, this guide has given you plenty of knowledge to continue forward in your effort to raise your credit score. No matter how bad your debt is right now, you can decide to lower it. Each action you take is going to lower that balance by a fraction, but that is a fraction lower than what you started with. When you continue with a pattern like this, you are going to be living debt-free before you know it. Thank you for using this book as your go-to credit score guide. Please leave a favorable review and remember that you can do anything you set your mind to when you take your financial status seriously!

References

Bond, C. (2019, December 5). *"No Credit Score: What Happens Without a Credit History?"* U.S. News & World Report. https://creditcards.usnews.com/articles/no-credit-score-what-happens-without-a-credit-history

Brozic, J. (2019, August 12). *"VantageScore vs. FICO: What's the Difference?"* Credit Karma. www.creditkarma.com/advice/i/vantagescore-vs-fico/[1]

Cautero, R. (2019, July 22). *"What's the Difference Between a Hard and Soft Credit Inquiry?"* The Balance. www.thebalance.com/the-difference-between-hard-and-soft-credit-inquiries-4693740[2]

"Credit Reports and Credit Scores." [PDF]. (n.d.). Board of Governors of the Federal Reserve. www.federalreserve.gov/creditreports/pdf/credit_reports_scores_2.pdf[3]

"Credit Reports and Scores." (2020, January 22). USA.gov. www.usa.gov/credit-reports[4]

Fay, B. (2018, May 21). *"How to Improve Your Credit Score: Tips & Tricks."* Debt.org. www.debt.org/credit/improving-your-score/[5]

---

1. http://www.creditkarma.com/advice/i/vantagescore-vs-fico/
2. http://www.thebalance.com/the-difference-between-hard-and-soft-credit-inquiries-4693740
3. http://www.federalreserve.gov/creditreports/pdf/credit_reports_scores_2.pdf
4. http://www.usa.gov/credit-reports
5. http://www.debt.org/credit/improving-your-score/

Gonzalez-Garcia, J. (2019, September 10). *Credit Score Statistics.* CreditCards.com www.creditcards.com/credit-card-news/credit-score-statistics.php[6]

Henson, S. (2020, January 8). *"What Is a Credit Report?"* Experian. www.experian.com/blogs/ask-experian/what-is-a-credit-report/[7]

Issa, E. (2018, August 21). *"How Costly Is Bad Credit? Many Don't Know, Survey Shows."* NerdWallet. www.nerdwallet.com/blog/finance/bad-credit-score-survey/[8]

Jayakumar, A. (2019, April 10). *"What Is Credit History?"* NerdWallet. www.nerdwallet.com/blog/finance/credit-history-definition/[9]

Konsko, L. (2019, March 27). *"Revolving Credit vs Installment Credit: What's the Difference?"* NerdWallet. www.nerdwallet.com/blog/finance/revolving-debt-worse-credit-score-installment-debt/[10]

Mayer, B. (2019, October 21). *"Does Credit Repair Really Work? — 2020 Expert Opinion."* BadCredit.org. www.badcredit.org/how-to/does-credit-repair-really-work/[11]

6. http://www.creditcards.com/credit-card-news/credit-score-statistics.php

7. http://www.experian.com/blogs/ask-experian/what-is-a-credit-report/

8. http://www.nerdwallet.com/blog/finance/bad-credit-score-survey/

9. http://www.nerdwallet.com/blog/finance/credit-history-definition/

10. http://www.nerdwallet.com/blog/finance/revolving-debt-worse-credit-score-installment-debt/

11. http://www.badcredit.org/how-to/does-credit-repair-really-work/

Mitic, I. (2020, February 18). *"Credit Score Statistics: How to Interpret & Boost Your Score."* Fortunly. www.fortunly.com/statistics/credit-score-statistics[12]

Resendiz, J. (2019, July 15). *"Average Credit Card Debt in America: May 2020."* ValuePenguin. www.valuepenguin.com/average-credit-card-debt[13]

"Sample Letter for Disputing Errors on Your Credit Report." (n.d.). Federal Trade Commission www.consumer.ftc.gov/articles/0384-sample-letter-disputing-errors-your-credit-report[14]

"Understanding the Fair Credit Reporting Act." (n.d.). Experian. www.experian.com/blogs/ask-experian/credit-education/report-basics/fair-credit-reporting-act-fcra/[15]

12. http://www.fortunly.com/statistics/credit-score-statistics

13. http://www.valuepenguin.com/average-credit-card-debt

14. http://www.consumer.ftc.gov/articles/0384-sample-letter-disputing-errors-your-credit-report

15. http://www.experian.com/blogs/ask-experian/credit-education/report-basics/fair-credit-reporting-act-fcra/

Image Sources

800 (n.d.). https://unsplash.com/photos/TEYrLTKKMSg

Circle (n.d.). https://unsplash.com/photos/0a5VbkqqFFE

Credit Card (n.d.). https://unsplash.com/photos/em37kS8WJJQ

Do Not Enter (n.d.). https://unsplash.com/photos/gujgDy73Oh0

Fast Car (n.d.). https://unsplash.com/photos/iRnUeA04kUY

Fear (n.d.). https://unsplash.com/photos/cugryvziO_M

Five (n.d.). https://unsplash.com/photos/fYTfOzaRVWw

Frame (n.d.). https://unsplash.com/photos/3_Xwxya43hE

Graph (n.d.). https://unsplash.com/photos/AT77Q0Njnt0

Grave (n.d.). https://unsplash.com/photos/wxuPH6QRvJc

Laptop (n.d.). https://unsplash.com/photos/kUqqaRjJuw0

Numbers (n.d.). https://unsplash.com/photos/yD5rv8_WzxA

Percentage (n.d.). https://unsplash.com/photos/f4yVFrvSuHc

Question Mark (n.d.). https://unsplash.com/photos/VW-pFREtl0k

Reports (n.d.). https://unsplash.com/photos/hpjSkU2UYSU

Rocket (n.d.). https://unsplash.com/photos/UzOKDfoRrDU

Studying (n.d.). https://unsplash.com/photos/6RTM8EsD1T8

Tools (n.d.). https://unsplash.com/photos/9OKGEVJiTKk

Trophy (n.d.). https://unsplash.com/photos/_XTY6lD8jgM

Western (n.d.). https://unsplash.com/photos/ywVLrYtNXMQ

www.ingramcontent.com/pod-product-compliance
Lightning Source LLC
LaVergne TN
LVHW022102200926
848481LV00003B/1048
* 9 7 9 8 2 1 5 9 4 8 4 3 9 *

Table of Contents